Psychic
Self-Defence

Psychic Self-Defence

Spiritual Prescriptions for Inner Peace

Samantha Stevens

INSOMNIAC PRESS

National Library of Canada Cataloguing in Publication Data

Stevens, Samantha, 1960-
    Psychic self-defence: spiritual prescriptions for inner
peace / Samantha Stevens.

Includes bibliographical references.
ISBN 1-894663-50-0

1. Aura. I. Title.

BF1389.A8S72 2003   133.8'92   C2003-904490-4

The publisher gratefully acknowledges the support of the Canada Council, the Ontario Arts Council and the Department of Canadian Heritage through the Book Publishing Industry Development Program. We acknowledge the support of the Government of Ontario through the Ontario Media Development Corporation's Ontario Book Initiative.

Printed and bound in Canada

Insomniac Press
192 Spadina Avenue, Suite 403
Toronto, Ontario, Canada, M5T 2C2
www.insomniacpress.com

The Canada Council | Le Conseil des Arts
FOR THE ARTS | du Canada
SINCE 1957 | DEPUIS 1957

ONTARIO ARTS COUNCIL
CONSEIL DES ARTS DE L'ONTARIO

This book is dedicated to the staff and members of the Psychic Realm.

Table of Contents

Chapter One

Psychic or Psycho?

What is Astral Attack?

An astral attack can be simply defined as any kind of bad energy sent your way with the intention of, at the very least, ruining your day, or at the most, your life. This energy can originate from another person, a group or cult, a dead or living spirit, entities, elementals, objects or even yourself in some way.

The latter is particularly true of those who have been messing around in black magic or attempting to manipulate events through their thought processes. There is no better way to invite bad energy upon yourself than by purposefully sending bad energy to another. "Curses have a way of coming home to nest," as the saying goes.

Obsessive, fearful and anxious people, in particular, seem to invite astral attack on themselves as they are always subconsciously inviting "the worst that can happen" into their realm of possibility. They want so desperately to change events that their aura—the membrane that protects the soul—actually grows thin and exposes them to danger. Hatred is like a virus. It not only poisons and infects the aura of the person that you are attacking, it is also the spiritual equivalent of "shitting in your own backyard."

There are people who are psychic predators without even realizing it. Alcoholics, addicts, manic-depressives, depressives and people with similar disorders often cannot sustain themselves on their own energies. They become expert at invading the thoughts, minds and auras of others, simply because they need to drain others of their energies in order to survive. Some are so adept at developing a sixth sense that compensates for the ravages of their disease (lack of perception, damaged gut instincts, irrationality, desperation, bad judgment) that you can literally feel like they are sticking a hose into your gut and sucking your will to live. Sometimes you have no choice but to deal with such a person in your life. As a result, you may be in need of constant psychic protection.

Healers, mediums, psychics, priests, nuns, nurses, artists and those who open up the self to sense impressions, are vulnerable to astral attack. It is easy to pick up thoughts or spirits when you are working in a place such as a hospital, doctor's office or funeral home. If you find yourself working in such an environment, you are probably in need of some regular cleansing ritual that strengthens your psychic protection. You may unknowingly take home your client's or patient's thoughts or feelings.

Most astral attacks take place at the subconscious level. They originate as thoughts. One of the clichés that describes this process is the ripple-on-the-pond effect. The negative thought is like a rock dropped into water; the vibrations are eventually felt on distant shores. Another commonly used metaphor is the butterfly in a Brazil forest that flaps its wings and then causes an earthquake in Taiwan. Never under-estimate the power of a thought. That is why it is so important to stay away from negative people. As Florence Scovell Shinn says, "The Word is Your Magic Wand." Keep your thoughts positive and no harm shall be done.

However, before you leap to the conclusion that you are under psychic attack, it is important to realize that there is a fine line between psychic and psycho.

Many times people have come to me for a reading, absolutely convinced that someone is somehow calling to them as soulmates. Usually this "soulmate" is an ex. They will state the person is coming to them through dreams, coincidences and obsessive thoughts. More than half the time, this is the product of a deep neurosis on the part of the dreamer. The subconscious mind constantly tries to sabotage the conscious mind with drives, both sexual and death-realted. What these dreams or haunting feelings usually reflect is the desire of that person to be with his or her ex.

Many will also claim to be under psychic attack from a person that they actually desire. Or they will send bad energy to another individual and claim that person is actually attacking them. This is called a rationalization, not a psychic attack.

There are major differences between obsession, possession, neurosis and psychic attack. Although obsession is considered a symptom of psychic attack, it is not always because the other person is sending you bad energy. In fact, the person may not be sending you any energy at all. Obsession is part of the denial stage of the grief process and you may simply be courting this delusion to avoid the inevitable acceptance that the matter is over.

Formally, possession means that your aura has been entered by another spirit. Individuals who have died yet come to life again on the operating table often are said to be invaded by what is called "a walk-in." A walk-in is an opportunistic spirit, good or bad, that has taken the opportunity to slip into the dying person's aura and inhabit it along with the original person's spirit. A walk-in is not necessarily a bad thing. In fact the purpose of many religions that deal with mediumships (Tibetan Buddhism and Santeria in particular), is to reach a state of trance, stillness and near death that welcomes the invasion of a spirit into the body. These spirits are often courted and trained to assist in healing and manifestation practices.

A psychic or astral invasion is also not necessarily the result of a deliberate attack. Some people, whether they are healers or not, are just more sensitive than others. Like psychic sponges they soak up emotions, energies and impressions from people or places. Such individuals often feel depleted by over-interaction with people.

Some experience what is called a psychic attachment. This is when a thought form attaches to a person or is embodied in an object or a place. It is like we have picked up bad vibes that stay with us.

Psychic invasion can also be caused by geopathic stress. Buildings located on massive rock forms that are scientifically proven to hold enormous amounts of electromagnetic radiation, or on known energy vortices or ley lines, or above underground streams are thought to contain vibrations that shatter or weaken the aura. Some psychics or healers may deliberately choose to locate themselves at such a site where the veils between the natural and supernatural worlds are thinner. Also such locations are thought to be portals to other realms and hold the memories or psychic energies of events that have taken place there previously.

An emotional upheaval or a tragedy can also cause geopathic stress. Places where there have been rapes, murders, slaughters or wars are said to carry the spirits of the unburied dead. Such sites weaken the aura of the human visitor and make the person more prone to malfortune.

That is why it is important for you to follow your gut instincts. If you feel that a place has "bad vibes" or is filled with toxic energies (human or not)— LEAVE. Most of us are born with healthy auras that nudge us with physical and emotional symptoms if the energies around us are bad.

Another form of attack discussed in more esoteric circles can be loosely described as possession by energies that are not of this planet. The idea is that humankind actually began as the starseed of explorers from other planets, and that occasionally our alien forefathers send down relatives to check up on us. Apparently, the favored method of astral attacks by aliens is to implant objects that resemble black boxes or squiggles in the human's aura. These implants are thought to work like batteries that feed on negative energy and draw malfortune to the individual.

If you are reading this book it is possible that you feel yourself to be under astral or psychic attack in the present or feel that you have been damaged by an attack in the past. Or you might simply be looking for ways to strengthen your astral protection to safeguard against the negative energies that you sense are out there. Since the horror of the terrorist attack on the Twin Towers in New York City on September 11th, more and more people have come to acknowledge that the last thing the world needs now is more negative energy. Psychics describe that event as a time where a psychic veil, separating good and evil, was ripped apart and torn down. The idea that an event like that could even manifest was evidence that somehow the collective wish for good had been internally weakened by the usual culprits—desire for power, envy and greed. Like a forest of tuning forks, negative energies or thoughts tend to breed or cluster together, according to the principle of "like attracts like." That event was so horrific it caused mass damage to our collective auras and instilled the kind of fear and apprehension that is antithetical to the psychic health of any individual. As a result, those already damaged auras became worse after 9-11. It is your responsibility, as a human being who is evolving constantly in this Aquarian age, not to let yourself be pervaded or invaded by these prevailing negative psychic trends.

In these pre-apocalyptic times, it is more important than ever for humanity to raise the vibrations of the collective unconciousness. This is why it is important to ground yourself, strengthen your aura, conquer your fears and raise your own vibration to a positive level. Humanity can only be healed as it historically always has—by example and through one person at a time.

The Evil Eye

The Evil Eye has been around since the beginning of time. It simply means sending someone a thought that seems intrusive or invasive or has the power to hurt him or her. Bad fortune is thought to be the result of envy. The evil eye is not necessarily intentional or associated with witchcraft or sorcery. Oddly enough, this thought form can actually be complimentary in nature. The concept originated in the Middle East and Mediterranean, and was introduced into the Americas, South Pacific Islands, Asia, Africa and Australia by European explorers.

Sending someone the evil eye comes from the concept that we all have a Third Eye, located in the center of our forehead. Blinding, fogging or obscuring the Third Eye is often the intent of the energy's sender. Most of us have experienced the weird power of this phenomenon. All it takes is a gaze that seems to be unfriendly, indifferent or blank that seems to last a couple of seconds too long. Perhaps an image of the person staring at us preoccupies our thoughts occasionally for the rest of the day. The British and Scottish term for the "evil eye" is "overlooking," which implies that a gaze has remained too long upon the coveted object, person or animal.

Often referred to as the envious or invidious eye, the evil eye is also known as *mal occhio* in Italian, *mal ojo* in Spanish, *ayin horeh* in Hebrew, *ayin harsha* in Arabic, *droch shuil* in Scottish, *mauvais oeil* in French, *bösen Blick* in German and *oculus malus* among the classical Romans.

The original belief is that any evidence of your prosperity (children, livestock, fruit trees) will be spoiled just by looking at your goodwill and hard work with envy. Ironically, the curse of the evil eye is thought to be provoked by inappropriate displays of spiritual pride or excessive beauty. There is a theory that celebrities suffer more personal malfortune than others simply because they are subjected to more "overlooking" and envy than others.

This superstition might have some grounding in evolutionary psychology as usually one animal is thought to dominate another simply by staring at it for too long. Psychologically speaking, staring or glaring at someone is officially considered a personal intrusion. Apparently, there is a fine line between casting a glance and casting a spell. In these post-*Celestine Prophecy* times, this kind of stare could be compared to an etheric laser beam or amoebic arm that rips open your aura. Others would describe the infliction of the evil eye as the projection of an image (such as the image of the person you have offended or hurt) so that you see only that to the exclusion of all other sight. In other words, you see that person wherever you go or feel that your life's events are always colored by your dealings with that person. Another symptom is the inability to proceed with ordinary, daily events without feeling somehow compelled to make things right with the person you have often unknowingly offended with your grandiosity.

It is common folklore that the evil eye has a dehydrating effect on its victim. Vomiting, diarrhea, problems with the blood and eyesight, impotence in men, clumsiness, stomachaches, dry coughs, itching, hair loss and dry skin are all thought to be physical symptoms of an evil eye attack. On the astral level it is thought to cause the drying up of prana, chi, life force and the easy flow of prosperity in life. Muddy, murky or poisoned vision that is somehow attached to the victim's Third Eye also accounts for the sudden inability to make wise decisions.

Almost everywhere that the evil eye belief exists, it is said to be caused accidentally by envy or praise. Thus the phrase "Pride Goeth Before a Fall." Certain Mediterranean and eastern cultures warn not to praise a child too much, lest it invite the balancing effect of the evil eye. A classic situation would be the barren woman who praises a newborn baby. One remedy for this inappropriate praise would be for the new mother to spit, to symbolically "rehydrate" the situation. Also, she may speak ill of her child to counteract the malefic effects of the praise.

The belief that individuals have the power to cast the evil eye on purpose is more idiosyncratic to Sicily and Southern Italy, although the belief has certainly spread elsewhere—to the southern United States and the Latin Americas. Such people are known as *jettatore* (projectors). They are not necessarily considered evil or envious, just born with an embarrassing talent that causes others to avoid them. In ancient cultures, if you were thought to be the possessor of an evil eye, you were often negated by a society that refused to meet your gaze.

Perhaps one of the most familiar preventative measures against the evil eye is the hand gesture. The *mano cornuto* or "horned hand" involves extending the pinky and index fingers from a fist. The *mano fico* or "gig hand" involves placing the thumb in between the first and second fingers.

Historically there have been many cures for the evil eye:

In Italy, the evil eye is diagnosed by dripping olive oil into a vessel filled with water. Prayers are recited until the droplets of oil no longer create an eye shape in the water.

In Eastern Europe, charcoal, coal or burned match heads are dropped into a pan of water. If the items float then the person is considered to be the victim of a curse.

In the Ukraine, a form of ceromancy or candle reading is used to diagnose the curse. Melted wax is dripped from a candle into a pan of water. If the wax spits, splatters, or sticks to the side of the bowl then the "patient" is considered to be under the influence of the malefic eye. Usually the patient is cleansed with Holy Water. When the dripped wax sinks to the bottom of the bowl in a round ball, the victim is cured.

In Greece and Mexico, the official cure is to invite the culprit responsible for the evil eye to spit in a vessel of the Holy Water that is consumed by the victim.

In Mexico, rolling a raw egg over the body of the victim is the antidote. It is cracked open and if the metaphysician or healer scries the shape of an eye in the yolks then the person is considered cursed.

In China, the remedy for the evil eye is the Pa Kua mirror, a six-sided mirror that is hung on the front door or placed in the front window to reverse bad energy back to the sender. Some of these mirrors are convex to reflect back the bad "poison darts" or "arrows" of multiple ill-wishers, and some are concave to reflect energy back to a known enemy such as a nosy neighbor. In Feng Shui, mirrors are often used as a cure-all to reflect negative energy back at all kinds of things—people, bad architecture, traffic, neighbors, physical obstructions such as trees or rocks or anything else that might be considered a conductor of Har Shui (negative vibrations).

In India, the mirroring back of the evil eye takes the form of small mirrors that are sewn, braided or crocheted into clothing. This mirroring back of bad energy is also familiar to practitioners of Wicca, Yoruba and Santeria. In India, the human eye is also considered the mirror of the soul. Indian women wear kohl or heavy black makeup to emphasize their eyes not only to shield themeselves from evil eye, but also to prevent themselves from accidentally inflicting it on others. In India, cords strung with blue beads are placed on newborn babies. When the cord breaks and the bead is lost the child is considered to have a strong enough aura to protect him or herself from the evil eye. Red cords worn upon the wrist or neck in general is thought to have a powerful effect against ocular malevolence. A silver charm called Eye of Buddha which references the Gautama Buddha is also worn against astral attack.

In Italy, gold, silver or gems carved or cast into the shape of the *mano fica* or *mano cornuta* are used to repel evil. The most coveted ones are made of red coral, but many versions exist today made of gem-stones and plastic. They are worn by men to protect against the withering of the genitals thought to be caused by the evil eye.

Also Italian in origin is the corno, horn or devil's horn amulet which is thought to protect against the same dysfunction. The women's version is made from a twig of red coral.

In Arab cultures, superstitious types wear an eye in the form of a stone cast in the center of a hand-shaped bone or metal charm. A common Egyptian charm is the Buckle of Isis which represents the men-strual pad of the Goddess Isis who was the nurturer of all living things. Stuffing a little prayer or spell inside a locket that is hung around the neck is the common European custom for protecting oneself against deadly gazes.

A lightworker such as myself might advise you to protect yourself in the following contemporary ways:

Always maintain the belief that nobody has the power to hurt you with a look. This, in itself, is a very powerful thought form.

Before you go out, imagine that your Third Eye is actually covered by something that looks like a small pocket mirror. If you are a psychic or a healer then simply close your Third Eye and don't open it unless you want to look.

If you are feeling haunted or upset as the result of a "look," press your thumb hard into the center of your forehead and imagine your Third Eye quickly flipping. Flick the energy away with your thumb and snap your fingers.

Always remember that what you resist often persists. The phrase "Oh, so what!" is one of the most powerful chemicals in the universe that you can use to dissolve negative energy.

Witchcraft

Witchcraft is one of the most popular and accessible forms used to practice psychic aggression today. I define it as any process where a ritual is used to willfully direct bad energy at an individual. This ritual can be employed by an individual or the result of a group mind. The basic intent is to control, dominate or bend the will of the intended victim. Not all practitioners use witchcraft in harmful or misguided ways. However, it is the weapon of choice when it comes to astral assault for followers of Minoan, Wiccan, Alexandrian, Gardinarian, Yoruban, Santerian, Tibetan Occultist and even certain prayer circles.

There are two basic methodologies that are used in witchcraft to practice psychic aggression:

Sympathetic magic where the practitioner uses objects such as poppets, candles or other charged objects to reinvent a simulacrum of the situation. The idea is that the repeated drama of a desired outcome will eventually manifest it on a larger scale.

A spirit attack. In this instance, the metaphysicist has developed the ability to summon and send spirits to torture the intended victim. This may involve the sacrifice of animals or offerings to a God or Spirit.

It is important to note here that a witch does not always look like a witch. Every religion in the world practices some form of ritual—usually with fire or water—that is intended to intrude and affect the destiny of the object of the ritual. Despite the progress of civilization, such rituals have become manifold and diversified prayers are essentially spells. Anyone involved in any religion is dealing with an intermediary soul (priest, seer, medium) whose sole purpose is to channel energies, spirits and entities from the supernatural world. Unfortunately, as long as humankind continues to try to manifest a God on Earth, there will always be a Hitler. Almost all black magic originates from the intention to make "things right" or restore justice to a situation for religious reasons.

Most people have an irresistible need to belong to a cult-like following or be part of a group mind that is larger than the individual. The pitfall of this need of human nature is that although there is indeed great power in group mind, absolute power almost inevitably corrupts. If you find yourself under psychic attack from a group mind—whether it be meddling AA members convinced you should find God, a coven of witches who suspect you had sex with one of their partners, or devotees of a Buddist cult who think you should give your energy to one guru so he can ascend to the next level of enlightenment—your best defence is to have confidence in the idea that such manipulations, even if well-intended, eventually have a way of destroying themselves.

Unfortunately, there does seem to be some scientific evidence to back up the idea that the prayers or wishes of a group often outweigh the prayers or wishes of an individual. Thus, the popularity of prayer circles on the Internet. However, when the positive intent is reversed to negative intent the effect is said to sometimes have deadly results.

Not all psychic aggression originates from an abyss of hate, envy, revenge and a craving to do harm and get away with it. Sometimes the ritual is done as the group or individual is presupposing what is best for you. The classic example of this is the mother who gets a break-up candle from the local occult shop to try to break up her daughter's marriage to an abuser. Another example is the individual who prays to a saint that her husband stop drinking. Whenever you pray, pray for that person's highest good. Otherwise, you may be preventing them from learning valuable life lessons or experiencing their karma. Unfortunately, many groups or religions have followers that consider themselves to be the divinely appointed agents of karma. The minute anyone approaches you and offers to take responsibility for your soul or claims to know what is best for your karma, consider it a psychic attack.

The problem with white magic is that although it doesn't intend to harm others, the energy that it draws upon for its positive purposes has to come from somewhere. Crummy, yet well-meaning metaphysicians are always drawing it from the wrong places. For instance, drawing energy up from the earth sounds good, healthy and organic in practice, but what makes white practitioners think that Mother Gaia can afford to support us in this way? As in the days just before Noah's ark, the earth is once again polluted with magic.

Psychic offenders who practice black magic essentially are extracting malefic energies from the etheric realms and directing them towards a victim. The victim's vital physical and emotional functions are affected until the perpetrator gets his or her way.

The following is a list of the most popular reasons why individuals and groups feel justified in practicing sympathetic or spirit magic. Most are based on what are called "baby fears"—fear of abandonment, smothering and starving.

• The desire to be unique or conspicuous—in short, the desire for power!
• The desire to destroy a rival in career or romance.
• The desire to eliminate opponents or business competition.
• Punishment for thinking outside the perimeters of the group mind.
• The desire to eliminate differences in political, religious, ethical and philosophical doctrines.
• Envy of others or coveting their talents, qualities, belongings and relationships.

There are millions of rituals and spells out there that can be obtained to accomplish these purposes. There are also as many schools of magic as there are branches on The Tree of Life. There is Gardinarian magic, Alexandrian magic, Santeria, Yoruba, Minoan, Wiccan, Tibetan Occult, Vajrayana, Aboriginal Shamanism and Chaos Magick. However, some of the more common of these rituals or spells have similar formats.

One of the most innocuous forms of astral attack is the presentation of a charged token or item that is meant to be a gift to the victim. This object may have been prayed over, or contain a spirit that is intended to attach the energies of the victim to the group. Beware strangers bearing gifts. Over-familiarity and charm is the first line of attack of the witch or the shaman. Gifts are often given to create a sympathetic link to you.

Also prevent anyone who you suspect of astrally attacking you from entering your home, fondling or touching your personal objects. Especially avoid giving them a photograph and never let them in your bathroom where they may have access to items such as a lock of your hair. Also, do not let them know your full name or birthdate as this information can be used to make a ritual more accurate.

Any of your personal body fluids or items may be used in sympathetic magic. Usually these objects are placed around candles or used to create a poppet. A poppet is an image made in your likeness that is intended to represent you. Like a voodoo doll it can be stuck full of pins, thrown into flames, placed in a bottle, bound with ribbons or thrown into the freezer. The intent of these rituals is to hurt, burn, trap, stop and paralyze you in your tracks.

Witches of any sort also recognize the power of the word and its impact on the collective unconscious. Incantations may be used to affect the vibrations around you. For this reason it is important to keep suspected practitioners on a "need to know" only basis with regards to your personal life.

Another form of attack is the ritual that is performed to appeal to God or a specific god or goddess to invoke wrath upon your head. This is done using candle burning or offerings in a place of worship or at a graveyard. Sometimes a medium is used as a conduit for those energies that will be sent to the victim. If it's any comfort, usually the practitioner is indebted to the god or goddess for life for such favors.

The most malevolent and powerful form of attack involves the invocation of spirits. In most schools of magic this is done using a cast circle or talismans from the Book of Solomon. In Yoruba and Santeria the same is accomplished using offerings to ancestors and dead beings. The idea is to disturb the dead and instruct the spirit to bother, attack or haunt you. By ritually sacrificing living beings they summon inferior entities called "elementals" or demons—the so-called "spirits of Hell." Wicked entities then become docile, performing the witch's commands to bring about the suffering of the astral target.

In certain Celtic cults of magic, spirits are summoned from nature and are called elementals. Drawing down a spirit that deals with fire, for instance, might cause you to be plagued with toothaches, fevers, flashes in the pan, inflamed passions, bad tempers and relationships that suddenly end.

Egyptian, Celtic, Yoruban, Santerian and Buddist occultists are highly experienced in the art of creating a thought form. For instance, an experienced Tibetan occultist can use shakti or root energy to bring an evil thought into existence. This is one of the creepiest forms of magic and the hardest for the healer to diagnose as a problem. This practice involves the misuse of meditation and manifestation techniques to create an energy or actual life form from out of the ethereal matrix. The earth is actually polluted with thought forms that are the product of twisted minds. A well-trained yogi can actually manipulate or shatter objects from a great distance by creating the metaphysical equivalent of a poison arrow. Also, Buddhist shamans and witches are adept at using their powers to invade individuals through their chakras. One common approach is to visualize a hologram of the desired situation and then open the victim's crown chakra. This is all done with thought forms.

Some rituals involve the visualization of hooks, knives, arrows, daggers and darts into the victim's body. In sympathetic magic, this might actually be acted out using a poppet or a voodoo doll.

Another common format uses your own energy against you. Usually known as a "binding spell," this kind of magic can involve the winding of cords around a photograph, picture or poppet of the victim. Highly experienced metaphysicians can do this using malevolent visualizations: a ton of bricks falling or walls with steel spikes closing in on you. They might try to create some form of a "Devil's Snare": the more you try to use your own energy to fight against the prevailing trends, the more the energy will constrict and immobilize you.

Binding is used in everything from curses to love spells. You can use binding magic to do something (for example, attract good luck) or not to do something (stop smoking). You can bind a person to a person, an object to a person, or a person to an abstract concept, or any combination of the three. Not every binding is bound to a person. Sometimes "cursed objects" are bound to prevent them from harming another. This is, by far, one of the most misunderstood techniques of witchcraft. Many witches don't consider magic "binding magic" unless a string or cord is used. Thus, they think it's performed rarely—but behind the scenes on the astral plane, I'd say that at least half of modern spells in existence use binding of some sort.

Most witches don't get close enough to their victims to practice a direct psychic attack. When they do, drugs, alcohol and other substances are commonly used so that the witch can get close enough to you to develop a sympathetic connection or even do a ritual with you sitting in front of them. For instance, a coercive love spell might be to light a glass of rum on fire and then get you to drink it. In return, your predator would smoke a cigar. Little would you know that you are taking part in an offering being made to one of the goddesses in the Santeria pantheon.

The indirect psychic attack is more common. In most cases, people never find out that during a certain period of their life they were subject to some aggressive and destructive energetic emissions.

The worst thing about witchcraft is not only the damage that it does to the victims, but the damage it does to its aggressors. The issue of protection from the gods is huge in certain cultures, simply because it is acknowledged that there is no gain without some kind of pain. Psychic aggression is like cutting off your nose to spite your face.

What is alarming to me is the availability of the oral tradition and the number of dangerous amateur shamans and budding witchlets out there who are constantly creating negative thought forms and practicing black magic, yet constantly failing to achieve their aims. This energy is going somewhere, and often, like a misfired arrow from a bow, towards an unintended victim. Many times the aggressor takes action while in a state of emotional panic, which is antithetical to the practice of focused magical protocol.

The evil in this world is not due only to human stupidity and weakness. It is the cumulative effect of malevolent entities that have been summoned up by these practitioners. They feed off of negative emotions and energies. These entities tend to urge people to produce bad energy for themselves, and those around them. The typical amateur shaman or witch is highly receptive to negative suggestions and are encouraged by these thought forms to put magic into action without regrets.

Even people who do not believe in witchcraft can be a victim of this astral pollution. Telepathic induction is a hallmark of the witch's aggression. The victim that is not aware often passively bears the malignant energy sent to him. The consequences of this dirty practice may be: death, mutilation, accidents, psychic destruction, ruin of health, or loss of dear persons, assets or relationships.

Genuine psychic attacks that are the result of ritual magic are rarer than the more abstract kind, but the following are examples of evidence that you may, in fact, be under attack:

• Any symbol painted or drawn near the entrance of your home.

• Missing personal objects from your home such as a lipstick or hairbrush.

• Bones tied together with colored threads.

• Lemons that appear to be pricked with needles or nails.

• Garbage near your doorstep that is not yours.

• Pieces of bread that appear to be soaked in liquid.
• Eggs or eggshell pieces appearing in mysterious places.
• Round or square pieces of paper with numbers or symbols on it tucked in a place near your home.
• The remains of coconuts, eggplants and other fruits and vegetables near your home.
• Potatoes that appear to be hollowed out.
• Scorch marks on the sidewalk near your home.
• Dead frogs or other animals near your home.
• Photographs that have been ripped in two or pricked.
• Candle drippings of unknown origin.

No matter how "realistic" we may be, we have to observe the coincidence of such "appearances" with the beginning of miserable periods in our lives. The person who suffers attacks by black magic experiences the following: depression, headaches (in the cervical region at the back of the head and in the occipital regions at the temples), faintness, nausea, hives, diarrhea, pins and needles, smelling strange odors, a tightness in the solar plexus, anxiety, hallucinations, clumsiness, vision distortion, inability to concentrate and impotence or lack of sex drive. Other symptoms include: phobia of known things, fear of leaving the house, nightmares, lifting your arms or arching your back while asleep, talking angrily to yourself, excessive hand gestures, losing emotions for those dear to you, obsession with coincidences, compulsive thoughts about death, diminution of the ability to perceive between good and evil, inability to make a decision, losing objects, poltergeist activity, problems with electricity or electronics, stopped clocks and watches, drained batteries and sudden accidents.

If you are suffering from five or more of the above symptoms it is possible you are experiencing an astral attack. However, physical symptoms should be checked out by a doctor before you assume the culprit is the occult.

If you experience the symptoms above, make a mental effort to detect the source of the evil you feel and identify the aggressors. You don't always have to fight fire with fire. Sometimes you can put a fire out with water. Ways to redress the situation might be counseling, meditation, use of affirmations and positive thinking.

If persons affected by psychic aggressions cannot succeed in annihilating evil by their own effort, they should appeal to people able to help them. Many doctors, psychologists, priests, monks, biotherapists, clairvoyants and parapsychologists can recognize the symptoms of psychic aggression and take measures to counteract it. However, a word to the wise: there is an impressively large number of impostors who claim to have the "healing gift." Magic is big business, especially on the Internet.

The servants of "white magic" pretend to be the opponents of the "devilish, black magic." But, given the fact that "white magic" brings about chaos in victims' lives by binding or splitting up destinies, destroying families and helping offenders escape punishment, it may be wise to conclude that all magic is black. The purpose of witchcraft seems to be to create a state of anti-grace, which suspends individuals and protects them from being granted grace according to the Divine Laws of the Great Being of Light.

Once again, remember, that what you resist, seems to persist. Your best course of action may not

be to attempt to fight group mind, but instead surrender the problem up to God or practice principles
of metaphysical transmutation (the transformation of
negative energy into positive.) However, in theory,
there is no such thing as negative or positive energy,
only energy that is misused, abused or generated to
create an imbalance in the universe. The key to
handling attacks that are the deliberate result of
witchcraft is to find a way to rise above it, so that it
has no effect on you. As witchcraft is an artifice,
something that is not of itself, it is easily negated by
the power of Divine Love. It is created by humans,
somewhat like theater on a stage, and nothing kills a
bad play faster than a lack of audience. As the sages
say, the opposite of hate is not love, it is indifference.

The Power of Thought Forms

The imagination of the powerless is the most powerful
imagination of all. For that reason, those who are
desperate seem to be the most adept at creating
negative thought forms. Their desires to bring certain
negative events into reality are further charged by
subconscious sex, death and primal drives as well as
negative emotions such as fear, doubt, anxiety,
anger and resentment. Negative emotions are the
energy that animates thought forms and causes them
to manifest as your reality. Many of the situations that
occur in our lives are simply Medusa's mirrors.
Mostly what is wanting in our own lives, is reflected
in the lack of love or support we receive from others.
Negative situations or people are reflections of a
Frankenstein we have created, and whose arrival we
have dreaded for quite some time. The Buddhists call

manifesting a bad event from foul root energy "lousy shakti."

The subconscious is also sensitive to words, so you should be careful about how you label or word things in your mind. There is a theory that negative words and language adversely affect the subconscious mind. People inadvertently curse each other all the time by fretting over worst-case scenarios and naming situations in a way that acts almost like the opposite of a positive affirmation. A good example is a mother saying to a daughter "If you don't lose weight, nobody is going to marry you." Statements like that, are in effect, subconscious curses, even though they are well-meaning in intent. For this reason it is important to avoid people who are critical in their speech or masters of verbal abuse. They weaken your aura and make you more vulnerable to psychic invasion and astral attack.

A major symptom of astral attack is having thoughts about one person, one guru, one matter or a single situation to the exclusion of all other thoughts. This is evidence that another person has subtly tampered with the language of your subconscious.

Talented channelers, shamans and witches can behave on the astral plane, much the same way a politician or the media does during a crisis. Through the process of naming, labeling and consistent visualizing, they literally campaign and lobby the gods, angels, devils and karmic wheel to warp reality to their liking. Whether or not such a consistent appeal works all depends on the strength and health of your aura and your ability to tune out their low-level vibrations.

Fortunately, most astral attacks of this type do occur at a mundane place on the spiritual plane. The best way to transcend these thought forms is to "surrender the problem upwards" to a Higher Self. Some refer to this as casting the problem upon "the Christ consciousness," or throwing it into the violet flame (a metaphor for the transmutation of negative energy into positive energy). The idea is to use your thoughts as tools to rise above the situation. Negativity has no power over you if you refuse to give it power. This process is usually reinforced with a variety of positive creative visualizations, prayers and mantras.

Our imaging faculties are quite powerful. This is why it is essential to keep our perspectives positive and realize that we have the free will to choose what we think about from moment to moment. Believe it or not, you are not at the mercy of your emotions or thoughts. You have the ability to clear your internal landscapes of any unwanted scenarios or guests. This is usually done through the practice of meditation.

My Personal Experience with Astral Attack

My own interest in this subject came about as the result of having to deal with a shattered aura. In 1987, I contracted a bad case of encephalitis (inflammation of the brain lining) caused by an allergic reaction to a spider bite near my ear. Encephalitis is a disease that slowly abnegates and shuts down your senses one by one. During the worst phase of it I had lost possession of all my five senses and came to know a mind void of thought that could be compared to years of accelerated meditation. It is during this phase of my life that I believe I rapidly developed a kind of sixth sense to compensate for the other missing senses. The disease also caused an electromagnetic shift in my body and I emerged from the experience as an epileptic. Until I learned to manage that condition, I found myself becoming a magnet for sordid events and plain bad luck. I quickly learned that prayer, meditation techniques and creative visualization could be used not only to heal my injured brain and body, but also restore a sense of astral well-being. I learned how to reverse the polarity of my energy so that it works for me, not against me.

My first experience with psychic attack occurred years before I contracted encephalitis, when I rented a haunted house on Richmond Street in Toronto. Whatever entity was in that house appeared determined to attach itself to me. At the time I was only twenty-four and too logical to actually realize that the experience I was about to embark on had all the markings of a true astral attack from the psychic world.

For one thing, I was obsessed with renting this house, even though it was in bad condition and would require a few roommates in order for me to afford it. It did not suit my purposes at all and yet I felt compelled to rent it. An irrational compulsion or feeling like this is one of the first indications of psychic attack.

Animal infestation is also a symptom of astral attack. In this case it was hordes of black cats. Every time I looked out a window, there would be four to five black cats sitting on the window ledge, looking at me. The manner in which these cats would appear was odd. For instance, some days, I could step out onto the porch and the yard would be empty. Then five minutes later I would step out and see one hundred black cats. This phenomenon did not manifest until after I had signed the lease. During the six months I lived there, I called animal control several times and the one time they did show up, there was not a cat in sight.

Once I rented the house, I had trouble renting a room to anyone. Technically I needed three roommates to make the rent. Person after person would enter the front foyer. Some did not want to step across the threshold. As I considered myself the female equivalent of Spock in those days, I put this up to the eccentricity of city people. Their gut instincts were telling them that the house had "bad energy."

During the six months that I lived in that house, I never once went down into the basement. I was irrationally afraid of touching its door handle. The ten or so roommates that rapidly moved in and just as rapidly moved out also never, ever once got beyond opening the door to whatever was down there. A thirty-five-year-old chef who moved in did open the door once, but could not bring himself to go down the steps. Once again, an irrational fear like this is a marker of psychic invasion.

The house also had several strange areas where one never felt quite comfortable. Something was definitely wrong with a spot at the bottom of the stairs. The floor seemed permanently discolored and I often tripped or fell on that spot, even though technically, there was nothing wrong with the floor. Another hot spot was the hallway at the top of the stairs. It was bordered by a railing and linked the three bedrooms and the bathroom. Everyone, young or old, male or female, was terrified to walk down that hallway alone at night even with the lights on.

Every morning around 1 a.m. I was consistently awoken by the sound of my bedroom door opening by itself. I would relatch it with a hook, but sooner or later I would hear the soft click of the latch falling and the door swinging open. Sometimes I would get up as many as thirty times in a night to relatch the door. I wanted the door closed because it gave me a view of the long dark hallway, and many times I would think I was seeing a large, dark shape moving along the balustrade. I also had the uncomfortable sense of being watched by things. Still I did not move out. I considered these things to be the product of sloping floors and an overactive imagination.

The first woman who moved in was a bartender and Tarot Reader in her thirties who seemed to be equally drawn to the energy of the house. However, on the first night, she called my name and asked me to meet her in the hallway to accompany her to the bathroom as she was afraid of something she kept thinking she saw coming up the stairs.

Night after night we kept hearing these scrabbling and scratching noises. We kept flicking on her light in her bedroom, suspecting it was mice scrambling up the side of her wicker shelving (even though it seemed impossible that there would be any mice at all in the place with so many cats around). Then one night, we were sitting, cross-legged in the dark waiting to see if we could catch what was making the noise, and we noticed fiery laser blue crackles of light, like shots of electricity, moving laterally up the south side of her wall. That night she slept with me.

Other strange phenomena began to take place. We could not keep a clock running in the house. No matter what kind of clock we bought, it would just stop within minutes of entering our possession. Tampering with clocks is a favorite pastime of spirits and entities. Finally I bought a state of the art, expensive hand wound clock with a lifetime warranty. One of the most frightening moments of my life was lying in bed and watching the hands of that clock stop and seem to jam at 1:05 a.m. Then the face of the clock began to rotate instead of the hands.

I also kept a chessboard on the coffee table downstairs. Every morning when I woke up a pawn was always missing from the set. The missing piece would turn up someplace odd later, like standing alone on the top shelf of a bookcase or behind a kettle. Although evidence was building to the contrary, I kept shrugging these events off as having some kind of rational explanation.

As I was a film student at York University at the time, I also was in possession of a lot of camera equipment. Throughout my stay there I could not take pictures inside the house. I tried taking photographs with several Nikons, a super-8 camera and a 16mm camera. Every single time, the single cell batteries in the camera would go dead. There was one day, determined to fight this, that I went through eight packs of batteries, simply trying to get a camera to work. It was like whatever was in the house was eating up the energy from the batteries.

The Tarot Reader and I went through a succession of about six roommates, all of whom fled the premises in less than a week. All were scared of the hallway and all demonstrated bizarre behavior. One friend of mine who moved in, a successful and normally cheerful forty-year-old theatre producer, sat all day on his bed, staring into space, aiming a toy gun at his head and clicking the trigger. A girlfriend of mine who moved in, a successful actress, became obsessed with painting every door frame and door jamb black.

She spent three sleepless nights obsessively outlining the perimeter of every room with black paint while on her knees, crying. She actually fled the premises in the middle of the night without informing us. This was truly out of character. These people are still my friends today and we still marvel at how odd that time was. Neither has any explanation for their behavior.

The Tarot Reader finally moved out after we watched an unseen hand pull all the clothes off the hangers in her closet one by one. The Tarot Reader was completely horrified by my decision to stay and despite her urgings I rented the rooms to yet another six people who didn't last more than a day or two.

In the meantime, I was suffering some strange phenomena at night. I would lie in bed and be disturbed by what I thought were the walls changing color. They would seem to be turning brown, almost in the same way that a matchbook browns when you toast it with a lit match. This started happening in conjunction with the door swinging open by itself at night. This kind of distortion of perception is also common with astral attack. When I woke in the morning, my clothing would smell strange, as if it had been soaked in gasoline. Some days I would wake up with what looked like bruises or bite marks on my thighs, belly or legs. Followers of the paranormal will recognize this as a spirit attack from what is called a *succubus*—a spirit that attacks women in the night.

Two new roommates moved in. One was a Filmmaker and the other was a Student of Philosophy. The first thing the Filmmaker did was decorate the premises with large posters of famous horror films. In retrospect, I realize he was feeding the energy that was already there.

The Filmmaker and I soon recognized a real problem when the Philosophy Student locked himself in his room for two weeks. He seemed to be in there with a tape recorder taping his voice and then playing it back. Finally one night he started screaming and we had to call the police. When they broke into his room, we found that he had been playing with cartons and cartons of eggs. He was booked into a hospital and diagnosed with a bad case of schizophrenia. In retrospect I realize his aura was weak and whatever was in the house, had cracked it open. Oddly, he was playing with eggs, which are a classic remedy for the evil eye.

They say that you are most vulnerable to psychic attachments when you are wet, as water is a conductor of psychic energy. There was always something a little bizarre about the bathroom which was the size of an entire bedroom and featured an elegant claw foot bathtub with an ancient shower head. There was a hole in the bathroom floor, the size of a peephole that allowed you to look down and see who was in the kitchen.

One bright summer day I was taking a shower and heard someone knock at the door. The Chef and the Filmmaker were home so I thought it was one of them trying to get in. I yelled "Just a second!" but the door kept thumping. I peeked out from between the shower curtains and watched as the doorknob rattled clockwise and counter-clockwise. "Can't you hear that I am taking a shower!" I yelled again as the door continued to shake and thump like someone was kicking the door from the outside. Furiously I stepped out of the shower, thinking one of the guys was playing a joke on me. I leaned down to look through the peephole in the bathroom floor where I saw the Chef and the Filmmaker happily cooking something in the kitchen. I screamed and unlocked the bathroom door. There was NOBODY on the other side. The Chef and the Filmmaker rushed upstairs, and we searched all the rooms. There was nobody there.

That night the poltergeist activity increased substantially. I had several friends over to keep me company because I was scared. Frankly, many of them thought I was losing it as I was now raving about bathrooms and ghosts and clocks stopping and things biting me in the night. Then in front of us all, a glass ashtray sitting in the center of the coffee table broke completely in half with both halves sliding in opposite directions on the floor. Then the chandelier in the living room, which had always made a lot of unwarranted tinkling sounds anyway, began to twirl in a clockwise circle. Everyone hightailed it out of the house, and that night I stayed at a friend's house.

It was the next evening before I finally made my way back home. I opened the front door, and saw an unearthly shaft of bright blue light rising from the floor at the spot in front of the stairs. Then I heard sounds upstairs like somebody was throwing large pieces of furniture around. I went to a corner phone booth and called the police. They investigated and found nothing.

That night I stayed at the Tarot Reader's apartment. I never went back in the house again. I left everything there, including most of my clothes, my futon and all my furniture.

The Filmmaker however, did phone me to say, that after the police were there, he found an antique dresser drawer of mine standing in the middle of the bedroom instead of against the wall even though the police and I had witnessed it as being against the wall. The theater producer called a psychic, who entered the house and immediately left because of bad stomach cramps. Stomach cramps are also a symptom of spirit attack. Without hearing my story, he confirmed that there was an entity that seemed to be linked to the bottom of the staircase.

Seven years later, I saw my antique bureau in a Salvation Army Thrift Shop near the house. It had been a beautiful, burnished walnut brown and was one of my prized possessions. Its carnelian handles were either cracked or missing, and it looked worn and bleached as if it had been tossed around in a salty sea. I avoided looking in the mirror, lest I make contact with whatever entity was responsible for so much misery again.

The above case is a classic example of what it is like to be the victim of an attack from a dead spirit. My insistence on not leaving is classic of those suffering from a psychic attachment. In this case, the dead spirit would normally be cleared out by a medium or ghostbuster. It took me years to digest the impact of this experience on my health and aura.

During a period in my life in the 1990s when I was a well-known pop-culture columnist, I found myself constantly dealing with what is classically known as the evil eye. A small measure of fame made me the object of numerous intrusive stares from strangers and also attracted many stalkers into my realm—four of whom were sent to jail. Being a little more knowl-edgeable about the way astral attack works, I always made sure that my face was obscured in my byline photo so obsessive individuals would have a great deal of difficulty hooking into my energy.

Whenever you obtain any measure of celebrity, you are always going to be the object of psychic invasion. By churning out a weekly column, I had broken a cosmic rule and was attracting undue attention to myself. The hundreds of letters that I received every week as a result of this column proved that many people had me on their mind at once.

When you are the focus of mass thought, it is important that you have a strong and healthy aura that is able to withstand all of the attention. Remember, even too much praise is considered a function of the evil eye. While publishing this column I often felt battered by unseen forces and also suffered incredible bouts of ill health that seemed to be the result of psychic attacks by readers. For instance, I suffered from teeth, jaw and mouth problems, possibly because there were many readers out there who wished I would shut up. I also found myself to be the target of envy as it seemed that everybody thought they could do my job better than me. To protect myself I avoided reading in public and actually spent four years limiting my time in public places to avoid paying physically for my artistic practices more than I thought I already had.

During my eleven years doing this job I first encountered deliberate curses. Usually they would arrive in the form of a letter in an envelope covered with symbols, sigils, magic squares and other things. Usually the letter would begin "As you begin to read this, this curse will now take effect...." My remedy for that at the time was to throw the thing in the garbage. However, such alarming astral threats became so numerous at one point, that it encouraged me to step up my research into the art of Psychic Self-Defence even more.

Above I have discussed what it is like to be astrally attacked by the dead, but in recent years I have also experienced astral attacks from the living—one from an individual and one from an individual who belongs to a cult.

In the late '90s I went out with an individual who fits the perfect description of a "psychic vampire." When we first met, this individual courted and charmed me. I was interested in him because he displayed a well-rounded knowledge of magical protocol as well as talent as a channeler and a medium.

Although this individual was everything that I did not want in a partner, I let him move in with me. He was an angry, brain-damaged man and on disability. He did not pay rent and made it clear he never intended to do so. I was mistaking psychic empathy for true love. The fact that I felt sorry for him opened my aura to invasion.

Expert psychic vampires also know how to use physical touch to leave an astral imprint in your aura. In retrospect, I see that this individual used an erotic incident to hook into my third chakra and invade my solar plexus. The tie between us was invisible but formidable. After this happened, I could not stop thinking about him. His concerns became more important than my own. Even though I am a big believer in The Rules, I found myself calling him four or five times a day to check up on him. I was not his girlfriend, yet I felt somehow possessed by him. Later in the relationship, he claimed that he would practice little rituals to keep me tied to him. For instance, whenever he laced up his boots he would say, after tying the knot together, "this represents Samantha and I together." This is a crude, practical form of a binding ritual. During the courting stages of our relationship he also admitted to winding copper wire into coils while talking to me on the phone. Copper is the metal of Venus and copper wire is used in rituals to bind individuals to each other. Whether he knew it or not, he was practicing a form of black love magic.

This individual also claimed to be a shape-shifter and adept at astral travel. I believe it because of the number of nightmares I would have about him. In these nightmares I would always be searching for him, in room after room, but he would not be found. I soon realized that every time I went to bed, I was taking an astral walk out of my body. It was if my soul was searching for him. What was odd about this is that I was not even particularly attracted to him.

The first demonstration I had that this person truly did have some psychic abilities was when I dared have another man over to my house. This friend was also a channeler and the psychic vampire did not like the idea of him treading on his turf. This man woke in the middle of the night screaming at the spectre of a shadowy presence flying down from the ceiling and attacking him. He actually fled my home. The next day the vampire called and coyly asked me if he was gone. He then claimed that he sent a spirit over to "kick his butt."

My suspicions that he was fooling with my aura were confirmed when I went to the psychic fair to get my annual electromagnetic photograph of my aura. I did this every year and published this photo in my column. Usually my aura is a balanced, tall and healthy blend of green, gold, orange and pink. After spending six months with this person I was horrified to see that it had turned a blazing scarlet and that it had shifted about three feet to the left. He slept on the left side of the bed so I began to conclude that his energy was pulling my aura towards him even in bed.

He began to display signs of real madness. One day we were sitting in a café waiting for a friend of mine. He kept cursing and cutting up this friend, who did not show up as promised. When I wondered what could have happened to this person, the Vampire smiled coyly and said, "Oh don't worry, he's not coming. I keep visualizing him falling off his bike." The next day I found out that my friend did not show up because he had fallen off his bike and broken his arm.

A day later I kicked him out and began practices to deliberately detach myself from him. The more I did this, the more he called or tried to visit me. He could sense the withdrawal of my energy. About a month later he had a severe nervous breakdown that resulted in him leaving town. Still for months after I had nightmares and would often wake up in the most bizarre position—my back would be arched as if I was being pulled from a cord in my solar plexus up to the sky. A prominent psychologist helped me identify that posture as what happens when a spirit leaves the body of a medium. It is detailed in various famous works of art that depict possession. It took some time for his astral imprint to fade from my aura. Thankfully in spiritual matters, as in nature, time has a way of healing things.

The next individual who practiced a prolonged series of astral attacks on me was a Wolf in Sheep's clothing that—unbeknownst to me at first—was the member of a rather large, psuedo-Buddhist cult based in Edmonton and run by a former Baptist preacher. The first words out of this man's mouth when I met him were "I want to help you." A word from the wise: when someone is offering you help and you do not appear to be in any trouble, you are about to GET in big trouble.

Like most astral predators, this person used charm, flattery and gifts to initially get my attention. Among the gifts offered was an eleven-year history of sobriety (important to a person who doesn't drink), numerous contacts and projects to do with my career and, as he put it, "a chance to ascend in one's life." He kept spouting clichés at me like "when the student is ready the teacher appears" and making unsolicited comments about my aura or energy field. This is typical of the arrogance of most spiritual predators. They have the power to fix you and fix you but good.

He also gave me an "implant," the gift of a meteorite that had been held by the cult leader to keep in my possession. When he first gave me this rock, he informed me that it could act as a psycho-metric telephone, through which astrally we could communicate with each other. Sure enough, all I had to do was pick up this rock, hold it for a few minutes and the Wolf would call. We would basically communicate—medium to medium. This sacred rock had been charged with energy from the cult leader, but it also held a spirit that I could detect with my Third Eye. The object itself even resembled a Third Eye as it was round and had a hole in the middle.

The first night after I held the rock, I experienced what would be called an astral attack that is typical of getting involved with this kind of group mind. I dreamed that a group of individuals were lifting me out of my body and then operating on me while I watched helplessly from the ceiling. The most frustrating thing about this dream is that I could not get down from the ceiling and back into my own form until they were done.

The Wolf kept the company of two friends who were also members of this cult. They were an older couple in their fifties who spent some time in India and claimed to be yogis. At first I did simple things with these people, like take walks with them and go to the movies. Then I began to notice that their conversation was peppered with nothing but references to a man named John. At first I assumed that this John, whom they were so enthusiastic about was just as a good friend of theirs, until one day the Wolf took me to spend three days at their house. During that time we listened to tapes and watched videotapes of John speaking and channelling during one of his sessions. This got so ridiculous that at one point, the tape was always in the ghetto blaster that they carried around wherever I went. As all of them were recovering alcoholics, I figured they were substituting one addiction for another. Plus I have always been one to suspend judgment when it comes to psychic phenomena and appreciate those who at least appear to be seekers of Truth.

The Wolf often came over to my house to play videotapes of John and as I watched him speak on tape I realized that a strange phenonomen was taking place around my crown chakra. It was like he was taking a can opener to my crown chakra, opening it and then removing something. Every time after watching John operate on tape I noticed that this feeling—like having the top of my head sliced off as if it was an egg—was getting stronger and stronger. On the videotape, the cult leader was not saying that much—spouting well-worn clichés from the truth seekers of the 1920s and mixing it in with a bit of Jungian psychotherapy along the lines of William Pen Rock or Sanaya Roman.

Over the next two months Wolf's personality container also seemed to be collapsing. More and more the point of his existence seemed to be to emulate John's language, posture and the way he would persistently and blankly stare at people. Wolf eventually became famous for his "meditation displays" which involved closing his eyes and meditating in the most inappropriate of circumstances. He also began introducing himself to people as a shaman.

As I began to get to know these three people better, they finally began to confess to me that they believed that John was an alien or even Jesus Christ. Mixed in with all this was the promise of projects, travel and a future with the Wolf.

Then much to their dismay, several stories broke out in the Canadian media denouncing this cult leader as a fraud and bigamist who had left his wife and was now carrying on with a couple of young women. At this point, I began to question what kind of channeling this individual was doing and why it was necessary for him to invade our crown chakras. My queries were met with verbal criticism. Whether I liked it or not, I was slowly getting on the wrong side of these people, simply by being myself. I kept insisting that I did not need John to connect with my Higher Self. I also did not see the panic about wanting to ascend in one's life. To me there was something corrupt about spinning the karmic wheel faster and faster, as if it was the tire of a bike.

About three months after being given this rock to hold, Wolf relapsed after maintaining eleven years of sobriety. Along with this relapse came the usual lying, stealing and objectionable behavior. He would disappear for weeks and then claim to have the power of bi-location that was allegedly attributed to the master. My attempts to tap into his energy usually led to severe nightmares. I had one where he turned to me, said, "You're not holy," then he changed into a snarling wolf and bit me.

The relationship officially ended after Wolf and his friends left me behind after promising to take me to see John in person in Montreal. After months and months of psychologically preparing me for such an event, it was a letdown to be left behind. This behavior is also typical of cult members who practice negation of the individual who shows skepticism or who is not going along with their beliefs. They know that social ostracism makes one want to join the cult even more.

When the three of them returned from Montreal, my worst nightmare had been realized. According to them the cult leader had appointed Wolf as a disciple. This only served to increase Wolf's spiritual arrogance. Before I knew it, he was back in full-blown addiction. The yogis justified this by saying that John was stripping him down so that he could reach rock bottom. They were also happy that the female yogi had died two times while on a mountainous excursion so that she could be a "walk-in" for John.

After the end of this relationship, I had trouble disconnecting from their energy, even though I had returned the main transmitting device—the rock, back to Wolf. The energy that had seemed so divine, tender and graceful was now reaching me in tidal waves of malevolence and betrayal. My life was filled with malfortune: I lost my job, I lost teeth (teeth represent the foundation of faith in spiritual terms) and could not seem to make ends meet. I also began to obsess about both John and Wolf to the exclusion of all other thoughts. It almost felt like I was constantly being sent reminders to think of nothing but them. I began to experience nightmares that consisted of such scenarios as having my head shaved by groups of Freemasons. I was also experiencing demonstrations of astral attack in the form of crystal balls and lava lamps shattering. At one point, my electric juicer turned on by itself in the middle of the night. My collection of fountains stopped working and one of them began producing a rancid-looking foam. A friend of mine also began to have horrific dreams— one of which involved Wolf asphyxiating her to death with spray paint. That dream was probably meant for me but missed its target. My aura was getting thinner and it became harder for me to read people professionally as I could not discard the spirits as easily as before after I was done talking to them. The result was that I had a house full of dead people. I was also becoming an astral sponge—too easily feeling the emotions, despair and anger of my clients. I felt like I was turning into a walking, talking, living battery who solely existed for the purpose of feeding Wolf energy.

Finally, Wolf called me on the phone and accused me of witchcraft. He said that he had been sitting around with individuals on the astral plane, communing with them and that he was told to inform me that I was surrounded by toxic energies. (He was probably referring to my friends, members of the press that I knew and an ACA group I had joined to deal with his relapse.) He told me that if it was not me then someone had appropriated my astral identity. He then accused me of being responsible for the fact that his brother had been in a car accident. I took a cue from my experience as a reader of over fifteen thousand individuals and recalled that almost always, the person who is accusing the other of witchcraft is practicing a form of it. The accusation comes from a deep paranoia that you might be practicing a form of retaliation. This can be compared to a criminal returning to the scene of a crime to check if the corpse is really dead. At this point, I decided to try to get professional help. It was clear to me that these people were trying to short-circuit my natural ability to connect with God.

I cannot reveal what I did to escape from this situation, ultimately, as I feel I am still vulnerable to the energies of these people. However, I did do a cutting of the cord ritual between Wolf and I to formally try to break the astral connection between us. As is the case with most astral vampires, Wolf popped up right in front of my face on the street the day after I purposefully cut myself from him. The reason this happens is because the vampire senses his energy has been cut and he wants to know what has happened to his power source. Although he chose to show contempt by ignoring me, as most alcoholics trapped in shame-based behavior do, he still managed to brush his shoulder close to mine in attempt to make physical contact or perhaps reconnect. His movements were stilted and zombie-like, and were likely manipulated by another force. The fact that he showed up at all just after a ritual disconnection (after six months of absence) was evidence enough for me that he was indeed feeding off my energy. He did not realize that I was practicing the law of non-resistance. You cannot negate someone who wants to be negated.

Further action I took put an end to his malevolent thought forms forever. I recovered the energies and spirits that were stolen from me by these people. However, I do not hold the cult leader responsible for the ethically idiotic actions of his followers. How they choose to respond to his effects on them is their choice and not necessarily his responsibility.

This last incident is an example of how psychotic behavior often comes hand in hand with psychic talent. They don't call psychics "wounded healers" for nothing. Often their talents are a compensating mechanism that has helped them sustain enormous amounts of physical, spiritual and emotional damage.

Dion Fortune—The Mother of White Light

Many of the psychic defence rituals that are practiced today were originally the brainchild of Dion Fortune. Dion Fortune is the magical name of Violet Mary Firth, a British occultist and author whose adventures repelling astral attack are detailed in her book *Psychic Self-Defense* (1930).

Fortune was a medium who was adept in ceremonial magic and one of the first authors to approach magical concepts from the points of view of Jung and Freud. Her first astral attack occurred when she was twenty-nine and working in a school for a woman who used yoga and hypnotic techniques to shatter Fortune's aura. This attack, provoked by Fortune leaving her job, left her a "mental and physical wreck" for three years.

Fortune joined the Alpha and Omega Lodge of Stella Matutina, in 1919, an outer order of the Hermetic Order of the Golden Dawn, which was founded by Aleister Crowley. When she decided to leave the cult she found herself under attack again, but this time from a serious heavyweight on the astral plane. S.L. Mathers turned from being her teacher to oppressor and Fortune suffered all manner of attacks imaginable as the coven exacted retaliation on her for leaving.

Anyone dealing with an attack from a serious group of heavies in a coven should read Fortune's *Psychic Self-Defense* as it describes in detail how she used white light rituals to escape punishment from the group mind.

She later went on to form her own group, The Society of Inner Light and became a psychiatrist who specialized in dealing with victims of psychic attack.

As a result of her experience with psychic attack Fortune concluded that hostile psychic energy can emanate both deliberately and unwittingly from certain people and that one can mentally fend off such energy. Her work *Psychic Self-Defense* is still regarded as the best guide in the world to detection and defence against psychic attack.

Chapter Two

How to Identify an Astral Attack

The Diagnosis

Like everything metaphysical, the diagnosis of a spiritual ailment is not what one could call a pure science. To make matters even more complex, an ailing spirit is often associated with an ailing body, leading one to ask, "Which came first, the chicken or the egg?" A weakened physical body is sometimes more vulnerable to psychic invasion simply because one's electromagnetic force field known as the aura is low. On the other hand, a mind that is poisoned with toxic thoughts often creates stressful chemicals and hormones in the body that further weaken the aura and leave the individual open to psychic attack.

There are also many levels of psychic invasion varying in severity from psychic invasion to psychic attachment to outright astral attack.

A psychic invasion is thought to occur when a thought form, entity, or astral imprint has entered the soul and permeated it like a virus. This usually circulates through the ethereal system and eventually dissipates like a bad cold.

Psychic attachment occurs when an individual finds him or herself somehow possessed by, obsessed with or overly attached to an object. Often this object is charged with negative energy from another place or time. It is also possible to get psychically attached to a place or for a place to get psychically attached to you!

Astral attack is usually the result of a venomous thought form or a direct attack on your aura using a ritual. Some metaphysicians send spirits to harm you with the intention of directly separating you from your Higher Self or faith.

Unfortunately, the diagnosis of psychic aggression is a purely subjective. A vote between you and the healer, Reiki worker, channeler, psychic, medium or priest that is consulted to get to the root of the problem decides it. To make things worse, the psychic business is riddled with quacks and poseurs who are more than willing to hook you into a program of psychic healing for a few bucks. In fact, I would strongly advise you to avoid any reader, psychic or healer that offers you an unsolicited judgment or statement about your aura as that is a common "sales hook" used to draw you in for more services. Anyone who approaches you and tells you that you have a damaged aura, need to reconnect with God or need spiritual fine tuning is in fact, actually practicing a form of astral attack on you. It would be classified as implanting a negative thought form, creating the kind of insecurity and fear that could manifest their unwanted diagnosis into your reality.

Whether you decide to consult a professional or not, it is important for you to remember that ultimately you are in charge of your reality, what you believe and think, and your spiritual accountability before God. If it is any comfort, the human aura, like the human body, tends to want to heal rather than destroy itself and most of us have the capability of healing ourselves by looking within and cleaning up our own internal landscapes. Just as "you are what you eat," you are also what you think. If you think you are powerless over astral events in your life, then you will be. If you think only the local shaman has the power to cure you of your ailment, then that will probably come true. You do not necessarily need a third party to clear you of an astral invasion or an attachment. The most that a healer or lightworker can do is try to show you a way out of the darkness. The actual light is within you, not from an external source. A strong belief in this concept is grandly life affirming and helps you strengthen your aura on the spot.

Historically, there are some tools that have been used to diagnose invasions, attachments and attacks. The most popular one is the pendulum. A pendulum is a chain or rope with a gemstone or cone-shaped piece of metal dangling from the end. The pendulum is passed over the patient's body to look for disturbed energy centers that might be the place of origin of the attack. Traditionally, if the pendulum swings in a counter-clockwise circle as opposed to a clockwise circle then there is a weakness in the energy field in that spot.

Ceromancy, the art of reading candle drippings, can be used in these kinds of diagnoses. Usually the candle is lit and dripped into a vessel of ordinary or Holy Water. Then the diviner reads the drippings. A candle, representing the person being diagnosed, may also be lit. Depending on how fast or slow the candle burns, how short or tall the flame is, and which way the smoke blows, a diagnosis is made about how much psychic pressure from external or internal sources is afflicting the victim.

Some Reiki or lightworkers may also use psychometry. Stones or crystals are placed on the patient's body and examined later for clarity and temperature to see if the person's energy field is fogged or weak. A Reiki master may also sense what is going on simply by passing his hands through your energy field. Other individuals may be able to see the obstruction in your aura and remove it using an *anthame* (a ritual knife), their hands or minds.

Kirlian or electromagnetic photography can also be used to take a Polaroid or photograph of your aura. I have found this modern technology to be the most efficient and practical way to diagnose an aura that is being pulled at or interfered with by another. Spirits in this kind of photography often show up as balls or clusters of light. Attachments or invasions can look like dark spots or pale patches. A healthy aura shows a thin membrane around its bubble of light. In damaged people this membrane is often broken and sometimes even non-existent. Much can be told also by the aura's shape. If it is too conical and tall, it may indicate an attack on the crown chakra. Auras that are too flat, truncated, shifted to one side or missing the symmetry that is associated with a healthy etheric shield are also indications of invasion, damage or astral attack.

Mostly, however, astral attack is largely diagnosed by its symptoms, whether that attack originates from an inner or outside source.

Physical Symptoms

Below is a description of some of the most commonly reported physical symptoms that can arise as a result of astral attack.

Migraines: The veil between you and the outer realms could indeed be thin if you find yourself suffering from repeated migraines. Migraines are a kind of electromagnetic disorder that affects all of the major perception centers. Migraine symptoms include loss of vision, an altered sense of smell and increased sensitivity in hearing. In turn, these symptoms could be caused by an external attack from a toxic thought form sent to you and meant to poison your aura. Also, the shutting down of the senses associated with migraines could be described as one of the Seven Circles of Hell. For instance, if an attacker is using a clay doll, it could be covered in any number of vile substances with the intent of blinding you or forcing you to smell a singular smell all day. This could be the result of candle burning, voodoo-doll work or vile visualizations. Your body may be trying to deprive itself of its senses and force you to look inside your internal landscape to detect the source of the problem.

Occipital Headaches: These occur at the back of the neck. People who are under astral attack tend to be under a lot of stress. Many who visualize astral attack often picture the person being bludgeoned on the back of the head. Banging the victim's head against a wall is also a common fantasy.

Temporal Headaches: These are sharp pains that occur around the temples as a result of someone visualizing your head in some kind of vise. They may also be manipulating a doll with pins or nails to achieve the same effect.

Sinus Headaches: These can be the result of doll work, where the facsimile of you is being sprinkled or buried in some kind substance. Witches use everything from coffee grounds to kitty litter for these purposes. Sinus headaches can also be the result of emotional transfer, as sinus trouble typically represents unshed tears. If you have caused someone a lot of grief, they may be sending you their unshed tears—

"now you feel what I feel." Sinus problems are also an alert that you may be dealing with a focused attack from a group of people.

Third Eye Headaches: This is more common in psychics and healers, and usually feels like a mild fuzzy pressure in the center of the forehead between the eyebrows. This can occur when one is trying to channel you with either a positive or negative message. Third Eye attacks are also common with assaults from a group mind associated with a religious group.

Jaw Pains: One of the most common statements made mentally about an absent individual is "I wish they would shut up." Certain malicious rituals and spells also involve the binding of the jaw in order to silence an individual.

Visual Disturbances: Distortions of vision are usually caused by shifts in brain chemicals that force you to see wide angles or zigzags of light. Astrally, this is commonly caused by a spirit invasion. This is something that a channeler or medium is more likely to experience than a non-practitioner.

Changes in Smell or Taste: An entity is usually responsible for this kind of symptom although someone playing with a voodoo doll can also trigger it.

Asthma: Many rituals and spells involve the visualization of the sucking of life energy or breath from an individual. Also the body may be naturally responding to what it perceives as an unseen threat. If someone is imagining you drowning, you could suffer from asthma. There is also an entire set of rituals that involve smothering an individual by placing his or her image in a jar and corking it.

Stomach Cramps: Stomach cramps often symbolize an attack from either a group or an entity. The stomach or solar plexus is the center from which we connect to others. When a psychic enters a haunted area, often the first symptom that they experience is stomach cramps. This may also represent an attempt by a third party to disturb or tamper with your gut feelings. Stomach cramps can occur when an obsessed individual is trying to put a hook into your third chakra to connect you to them against your will.

Nausea: An upset stomach is associated with all forms of psychic aggression.

Diarrhea: People who are being overwhelmed by negative vibrations or soaking up too much astral information from others tend to suffer from this ailment. It is an emergency signal that the aura is trying to cleanse itself.

Arthritis, Rheumatism or Restricted Movement: Both binding spells and freezer spells can cause an individual to become "paralyzed" and experience less mobility. A person may be trying to stop you from what you are doing or freeze you in your tracks.

Hives: You may be having an allergic reaction to bad energy being sent to you. This may be the result of a doll or simulacrum-type magic where an offensive substance is covering a likeness of you.

Impotence or Lack of Sex Drive: A sudden inability to "get it up" is the aim of many spells that intend to separate you from a loved one. This is usually done using candles, binding, freezer magic and the manipulation of photographs.

Burning or Pins and Needles Feeling in the Extremities: Unfortunately, this may be caused exactly by what it sounds like. Someone may be visualizing or using a likeness of you as an actual pincushion. This feeling can also be the result of an attacker burning a photograph of you.

Emotional Symptoms

Perhaps the most succinct way to describe the emotional effect of astral attack is having emotions that you don't feel belong to you. For instance, you may spend all day feeling angry, when what is going on in your life does not support your anger. You may feel inexplicably sad, aroused, anxious, elated, happy or even maniacal. Most people who experience this sense whom the emotion is coming from and usually their first instinct is a big clue. This phenomena occurs mostly in codependent relationships, where two individuals are overattached at the solar plexus or level of the third chakra. Experiencing this kind of phenomena means you have a true astral parasite on your hands. Almost always, this kind of attachment comes from someone who is living and has a history of upsetting your life. Alcoholics, manic-depressives and people with personality disorders are especially adept at this kind of astral invasion. Usually the object of the attack is an empathetic sort, and the invasion is not always intentional. Such forms of invasion are also common among parents and children.

Another effect of astral invasion or attack can be a loss of feeling towards those that you normally have feelings for. This could be the result of a binding spell, a freezer spell, or one of the thousands of Break-'Em-Up Spells that are out there in the public domain.

Generally, the loss of emotional control is thought to be a symptom of all forms of astral invasion. It is a natural reaction to a disturbance in your aura. For instance, if you are in possession of an object that makes you feel great sadness, perhaps it is time to get rid of that object. If thinking about a specific individual makes you angry, stop thinking about that person. More than 90% of the battle against astral attack is detaching one's self from emotionally charged situations, bad memories and anticipation of a drama. On an astral level, emotions tend to charge otherwise dormant situations or events. Also emotions lower your overall vibrations to their basest levels. According to the principle of "like attracts like," if you are demonstrating a lot of anger and grief you will probably attract situations and people who are similarly affected to you. Similar energy forms tend to aggregate in groups or clusters. The same is true of spirits. One way to resist this kind of effect is to not make yourself or your home a comfortable place for negative energy to take up permanent residence. Like most predators, if the spirit or thought form has nothing to feed off of, it will either starve to death or leave.

Psychological Disturbances

Anxiety is perhaps the most common psychological symptom associated with astral attack or invasion and is usually the result of a disturbed electromagnetic field.

Common types of anxiety that people experience while under astral attack are:
• The feeling that if they don't act on something right away that the world will end.
• An obsession with an object or a situation to the exclusion of all other thoughts.

• A sudden compulsion to go about one's daily affairs in a ritualistic or compulsive way.

• Attacks of panic or hysteria.

• Fear of the unknown, fear of known places or things, fear that one might not be able to handle what is to come in the immediate future, and fear that one might hurt others or oneself.

A ritual or violent thought form sent to you from other people can trigger these kinds of disorders. For instance, if someone has given you a car as a gift, and is uncertain about your ability to care for it, you might find yourself obsessed with the car. Or someone may be sending you a thought form in the shape of a monster or animal that you might be sensing as a threat. In certain Wiccan rituals, words are loaded with emotion and you might be picking up on the drama associated with that—these rituals are designed to cause anxiety. Other kinds of visualizations and rituals act like Chinese water torture and are designed to slowly but surely beat down your defences by creating consistently irritating situations. Also common are candle spells, where a spirit is summoned to give you no rest or no peace until you behave as desired by the magician.

Certain kinds of poppet magic can cause quirky effects in its targets including clumsiness, speech disorders, general disorientation, confusion and the desire to act out. For example, you might find yourself walking along the street, talking angrily to someone who isn't there. When an angry or jealous spirit possesses you, you might find yourself feeling those emotions more or displaying uncharacteristic behavior. Those under the influence of a badly done love or lust ritual could suddenly become unusually promiscuous.

The humorous thing I have noticed about love, lust and "come to me" spells is that usually the receiver of the ritual does not tend to become lusty towards the sender of the spell.

An inability to concentrate on anything could also indicate astral interference from another person. The person who is upset with you and targeting you, whether they are using thought forms or ritual magic, is usually agitated at the time. It is quite easy for you to pick up on that agitation and be too flustered to go about your daily work.

Developing an unreasonable fear of water and avoiding baths or showers is also a symptom of astral attack. Water is a conductor of psychic energy and your gut instincts are telling you that you are more vulnerable when you are wet.

Also common in cases of astral attack or invasion is the feeling that there is a knot in your stomach or throat. Usually this effects the person's breathing and speech patterns. I often hear this in client's voices when they speak to me indicating that they have been blocked in the third (stomach) and fourth (throat) chakras. In this case usually the culprit is a living, mentally ill person who has astral hooks in the client and is enjoying a consistent feeding of emotional energy.

Feelings of depression, low self-esteem and fatigue can also be blamed on astral attack. This is usually due to a leak in your aura. Many people create a hole in their own aura in the hopes that it will allow an inaccessible individual in their life to reach them easier on the astral plane. It is important to make sure that it is not YOU who is attacking due to a neurotic need to substitute a real relationship with a spiritual one or a desire to draw someone closer to you.

Astral attackers function by draining your energy which in turn causes irritation, fatigue and insomnia. Some people experience terrible feelings of restlessness and longing, or suffer from compulsive behaviors and thoughts. Often these symptoms are the result of an astral leeching, which visually can be described as hose with a sucker on the end embedded in your solar plexus. In this situation, you can become nothing more than a living battery for other individuals who have deemed it necessary to empower themselves by taking from you.

Sometimes a dream is just a dream, but there are certain structures to dream imagery that can indicate an astral attack:

Dreams that feature out-of-body experiences. This can be the result of an attack by a group mind who together, know how to lift your soul from your physical self and replace it, altered, back in your body.

Dreams where you find yourself humiliated or confronted by groups or a round table of people. This is also indicative of a group attack.

Dreams where you find yourself continually searching through malls and rooms for one person. This is one of those dreams that means the opposite. The person is with you, but your subconscious recognizes that the actual love in the relationship is missing.

Dreams where someone is kissing you or trying to suck your breath. This is a typical invasive dream sent by someone who is suffering from unrequited love for you.

Dreams that involve a great deal of water. Water symbolically represents psychic energy. Dreams that feature breaking dams or leaks may symbolize a leak caused by an attack on your aura.

Dreams in which you are being threatened and chased by monsters or animals. In most schools of magic, mediums are taught to create thought forms or guardian animals that can invade the subconscious.

Dreams involving weapons or appliance that directs a substance at your face. Many people use tools in their visualizations to direct bad energy at you.

Dreams of being smothered, drowned, frozen or asphyxiated. There are many spells and rituals out there that contain this kind of component that could be picked up by your subconscious.

Dreams where you are shown objects like notebooks, billboards or movies. Usually these artifices for storytelling represent a mechanism in magic where you are being sent a message.

Dreams where you are telephoned, but you pick up the phone and nobody is there. Usually, in a healthy dream, you receive a message. The lack of voice on the other line represents the secrecy around most rituals.

The purpose of an astral attack is to destroy the container of the personality so that it eventually cracks. In severe cases, astral attack can cause compulsive, morbid thoughts, disassociation from reality and hallucinations.

Spiritual Symptoms

Believe it or not, an increased interest in spiritual things, the New Age Movement, religion and the occult can represent a psyche that is suffering from astral attack.

When you are being drained by an astral attack you may feel the need or compulsion to heal yourself or supplement your energy by seeking a healer, channeler, guru or religious group. The very idea that you need this extra support may imply that your spiritual vessel is somehow leaking or been emptied. Although such support can be helpful, it can, ironically, also betray a deep lack of faith, not only in oneself but also in the goodness of whatever power is up there. Ironically, most people who are seeking spiritual guidance are actually fighting what they believe God or a Higher Power has in store for with them. It is a form of resistance to being on the "right" spiritual path. The plain fact of the matter is that most spiritual paths are uncomfortable and God may not be giving you what you want simply because it is bad for you. We live in a time that is dominated by the need to believe that we carve out our own futures. This belief that we are actually "higher" than our Higher Power is enough to cause all kinds of holes and leaks in our auras.

One important symptom of astral attack is the diminution of the ability to distinguish between good and evil. Long-term victims of repeated astral attacks often suffer a kind of moral malaise. They also frequently express a lack of faith in a Higher Power and in goodness. They will insist this is the product of logic, when this kind of existentialism is the result of spiritual fatigue because of third-party interference. The intent of most astral attack is to separate us from our will and our faith. It leads us to put our trust in groovy gurus and false prophets. Even if the guru or prophet is genuine, we cause damage to ourselves by failing to recognize that the vessel for the spirit is separate from the vessel itself.

Another spiritually related symptom of astral invasion is an increased attention to what I would call omens or signs. Sometimes this phenomenon is just a stage of the grieving process. A typical scenario is a woman left by her lover for another, who keeps thinking that she is receiving astral messages from him in the form of coincidences—the constant playing of a favorite song, seeing people who resemble him or have his name and other synchronistic encounters. This psychological glitch keeps the griever in denial of what really happened because she is not emotionally ready to accept the reality of it. On the other hand, a persistence of this kind of coincidence can mean astral attack especially if the messages seem malevolent. Often too, when a person deliberately weakens his aura in the hopes that it will bring him nearer to a lost dear one, other entities and thought forms attach themselves to the person, compelling him to more obsessive behavior. The absent person becomes like God—if the color blue was God, you would see blue everywhere. The same is for the object of obsession. You have let this person become your God.

Healthy individuals with healthy auras are not superstitious. They vibrate at a level of faith that is so high, not even witchcraft can harm them.

Situational Symptoms

If you experience any of the following situational symptoms you may be under astral attack:

Constantly Losing Objects: This could be the result of someone wishing loss on you on a consistent basis or you may be the victim of a ritual that was designed to disorient and confuse you.

Always Missing the Goal: People under astral attack usually find themselves working hard, yet constantly confronting obstacle after obstacle. Success is often right within reach and then snatched from grasp. This frustration is also a punishment built into many rituals and spells.

Loss of Prosperity, Health and Family: Many spells are done exactly to achieve that intention.

Monkey on Your Back: Victims of curses may find themselves confronting a long-term difficult problem—such as an ongoing court case or unsolvable health or financial problem.

Friendships and Relationships Ending Abruptly for No Reason: People come into your life and then leave with no explanation. This is a form of evil-eye transference. Sometimes a ritual has been performed to cause others to find you repulsive. In other cases it is the result of an implant or energy transference to your aura that other people's instincts interpret as "negative energy." However, it is not really your energy. It is an astral implant that has been sent to you from somewhere else.

Mirroring: This is an effect that causes others to immediately mirror your actions back to you in an unpleasant fashion. For instance if you comment on a person being overweight, five minutes later, someone comments on your weight. Some rituals are designed to accelerate your karma and create psychic pressure to make you feel lonely or like you need to get help from the attacker.

Attracting Accidents and Violent Situations: A repeated series of accidents or violence can be evidence of a ritual done by an individual or coven that is wishing you harm. Auras that have been weakened by consistent astral attack also tend to invite a multiple number of astral attacks from other sources. As I have mentioned before, there are many people doing witchcraft who are not trained in the art. As a result, their misfires hit innocent people. A person walking around with a weak, leaky or damaged aura becomes a sitting duck for these stray energies on the astral plane.

Environmental Symptoms

Some places just have "bad vibes." Most people can detect these bad vibes and use words to describe them like "heavy," "tiring," "exhausting," "dead" or "draining." Sometimes this is because the place is actually inhabited by entities or spirits that feed off of human energy fields. Other times it is the result of an astral imprint left by an extremely dramatic and negative situation that took place there, such as a murder or a rape. These kind of energies are also felt on the sites of old graveyards and places where wars have been fought and bodies left unburied after slaughter. In natural locations, these vibes can be attributed to the lingering spirit of a ritual done by a group.

In terms of Feng Shui, the ancient art of Chinese Object Placement, astral stress can be caused by the following factors:
• A front door facing a road with oncoming traffic.
• A front door facing a church, graveyard or other place of religious worship.
• A view that is dwarfed by a large building.

All of these factors prevent the easy flow of life energy through your home and affect the aura adversely. There is a huge relationship between the health of the aura and the art of Feng Shui. I do not have the space to elaborate on it here, but if you do feel that you are under astral attack, the use of fountains, mirrors, trees, fences and wind chimes can substantially lower your odds of suffering geopathic stress in urban areas. Bad energy likes to conglomerate in the dark alleys of our urban areas just as much as criminals do.

The following are the most common environmental symptoms of astral attack:

Constant Dysfunctionality: Chaos reigns. No matter how much you try to maintain order, the place constantly slides into a state of decay. Appliances, plumbing and other matters have to constantly be serviced or maintainenced. This could be the result of spirits playing tricks on you or the result of a ritual attack that has ordered the disintegration of your affairs.

Weird Odors and Smells: This can be an indication that your house is possessed by a foul spirit that was already there or that a spirit has been sent to you by a practitioner. It is also a sign of a weakened aura.

Problems with Electricity or Batteries: Some spirits and entities seem to feed off of electrical energy. Flickering lights, electrical shocks, appliances that turn on by themselves and batteries that die before their time are all symptoms of astral attack.

Stopped Time Pieces: Spirits from other realms exist on a plane where there is no time. In some haunted houses, it is almost impossible to run a clock that keeps correct time.

Unusual Light: Some spirits or astral imprints represent themselves by a glow or an astral shaft or light that appears out of nowhere.

Poltergeist Activity: Objects that move by themselves, mysterious bumping and moaning in the night and everything else you've seen in horror movies falls into this category. These could be the spirits of former residents that have been sent to you via a ritual. Poltergeist activity can also be blamed on an aura that has been weakened by trauma, negativity, envy and resentment. Poltergeists like to feed on negative energy emitting from humans. Therefore, if you suffer from jealousy, you are likely to attract a jealous spirit. Psychics or healers that have become overstressed from work may also be releasing negativity that manifests in the form of poltergeist activity.

Identifying the Attacker

Thought Forms: Thought forms tend to affect our lives on a more mundane level. That is because they tend to be sent by ordinary people. We may experience more day-to-day and practical frustrations. This kind of attack is usually from someone you know, with whom you've had an unpleasant encounter with.

The Subconscious Curse: This kind of curse usually comes from someone you know quite well and cares for you. They may even be praying for your well-being. A good example of this is the individual who prays for the person with AIDS to have an "improved immune system" when the disease itself is an overkill of immunity.

The Self-Fulfilling Prophecy Attack: This kind of astral attack is often stated verbally in the form of a negative affirmation like "You'll never make your rent unless you get a job," "There's no way you can write that book in two weeks" and "Your aunt had diabetes so you will probably get it too." Words like this have a powerful effect on our subconscious mind which, in turn, sets to programming the conscious mind to write a disaster script for ourselves.

Unsolicited Criticism and Verbal Abuse: This might seem obvious, but this is a form of direct astral attack. The Unconcious Mind is influenced by cruel words. Because they hurt we often repeat them over and over in our minds. When we do this we are subconsciously cursing ourselves with another person's words.

The Collective Wish for Failure: The more success-ful you are, the more you attract envy and jealousy, and therefore the ravages of the evil eye. There are many people out there who will happily congratulate you on your success and then go home and secretly wish that you would fail for once. This can be powerful if you find yourself at the mercy of a large group of people who are all wishing, simultaneously, for your demise.

The Psychic Vampire: If you feel exhausted, fatigued or drained just by encountering a person, then chances are that person is adept at hooking into your third chakra and sucking your energy.

If this person is always on your mind than it is possible that you have become engaged in an energy exchange with someone trying to dominate or bend your will to their way.

Live Hauntings: These astral attacks tend to take the form of obsession and the object of obsession is usually a lover. When healthy relationships termi-nate, those involved are still left feeling whole. Live hauntings don't usually occur unless the real-life relationship was vampire-like and codependent in the first place. The most likely suspects for this kind of haunting are addicts, alcoholics, manic-depressives and people with personality disorders because their auras are in a weakened state. Although there may have been genuine love at one time, with one partner nurturing and taking care of the other, these relationships often degenerate into power and ego struggles. Long after the person is gone, the person left behind often still feels addicted to that person. Or they feel that their presence is reflected in omens, coincidences and synchronicities that occur in their lives. If you are completely obsessed with an individual—if you see or feel their presence everywhere, you are most likely the victim of a live haunting.

Amateur Shamans and Witchlets: Sometimes you deliberately cross such people, other times they see themselves as agents of karma, and sometimes you don't know them at all. People playing with magic are a growing problem in terms of astral pollution on our planet. They are influenced by television shows, movies and the availability of spell books on the market.

These individuals are generally quite harmless, but they can cause havoc in one's life on the mundane level. If you have known no enemies in your life, are reasonably free of envy, resentment and fear and yet still cannot figure out where your haunting is coming from, it is probably the result of a thought form produced by an amateur shaman or witchlet. These attacks are not intentional, they are just the products of bad aim, unfinished rituals or lack of magical protocol in general.

Cults, Gurus and Group Mind: If you feel irresistibly compelled, beyond all rational reasoning, to join a cult, coven or religious organization, you may not be necessarily following your heart, you may be under astral attack.

Cults work by downloading information into your crown chakra. Victims often feel inferior, unholy or lonely if they do not join the cult. To determine whether you are under astral attack from a group mind, use this simple test—stay away from them for a few days. If you suffer extreme malfortune, then they are probably practicing some form of binding on you to keep you with them.

Also, if you are experiencing a run of bad luck, it is possible that the group has stolen your guardian spirits and are holding them hostage, so that you feel unprotected in any situation that does not include them.

Astral Imprints: An astral imprint is a bad memory that won't go away, but the memory is not necessarily yours. Astral imprints are left by people, dead or alive, in buildings or environments (like a graveyard). Living individuals can also leave their astral imprint on objects that they have touched or used during the time that you knew them. Antiques often hold the astral imprints of former owners. If you find yourself obsessed with an object or feel disturbed or upset while holding it then you are most likely dealing with an astral imprint.

Curses: If you find yourself living out the same karma again and again, or find that a tragic pattern of loss, illness or misfortune is often repeated in your family then you might have been ritually cursed at one time. Curses have a way of playing themselves out in an ironic pattern that the bearers find almost unfathomable in terms of its coincidence. A good example would be a family in which all of the fathers have died on the same date for three generations.

Repatterning for Failure: This form of astral attack is often the result of being involved in a cult or religious organization that has repeatedly told you that if you do not do follow certain rules, you will most certainly be punished. Often these slogans are implanted in the crown chakra which is open during periods when the group prays or meditates together. This is the equivalent of implanting an astral hologram in someone's consciousness that plays itself out the same way every time the individual attempts to resist the group's wishes.

Attacks by Spirits or Demons: If you are experiencing physical symptoms accompanied by poltergeist activity then it is possible that you are the victim of an individual or group who has summoned a spirit to persecute you until you bend to their will.

Attacks by Ghosts: This attack is usually accompanied by physical symptoms, most notably stomach cramps. As well, you might experience mysterious noises, poltergeists and actual ghost sightings.

Chapter Three

The Cures for Astral Attack:

Asking Politely

The Path of Least Resistance

The visualizations, prayers and other solutions in this section fall into the category of meditation or white magic and should be your first line of defence before you resort to the heavier stuff in the following chapter. They do the least damage to your karma and follow Christian and Buddhist principles of non-resistance.

The Bubble of White Light

The best way to prevent an astral attack or minimize its effects is to maintain a healthy aura. The simplest meditation you can use is the Bubble of White Light Meditation, which rinses your aura of negative energy and is effective against all forms of astral attack.

Relax. You can do this sitting, standing or lying down as long as you are completely relaxed. Breathe from your solar plexus—long, slow deep breaths. Now imagine yourself surrounded in a bubble that extends around your body in about three feet in all directions. Sense this bubble around your body. Is there anyplace where you sense a hole, leak or rip in the bubble? If so imagine yourself patching, sealing or fixing the hole. Each time that you breathe in imagine this bubble filling with a bright white light. With each breath the light becomes whiter and brighter. Do this for three minutes or more until you feel your body surrounded by this blaze of light. This light is blinding and obscures others from finding you within its depth. Now imagine that a membrane covers this bubble, somewhat like you would see on a soap bubble. This membrane is a mirror or impermeable shield that deflects all bad energy back to its source.

Cutting the Cord Meditation

This classic ritual is a good way to sever yourself from a psychic vampire or entity that you may feel is leeching energy from you. Sometimes, after a relationship has ended, many of us have problems letting go. Many of my clients complain of feeling haunted or even possessed by a dearly departed (who probably isn't even thinking of you and is busy with his or her new partner). It's like the person has left an indelible imprint upon your heart and you feel you can't go on unless the ex returns. The energy of the ex might be manifesting itself in all sorts of ways—in what you perceive as omens or reminders that occur in everyday life (such as a phrase or song lyric) or even as a visitor in your dreams.

There are all kinds of cures for this phenomenon (everything from burning bundles of sage to clear the room of the ex's vibe to throwing out every single reminder of him or her, including the bed). Yet before you ditch the Sealy Posturepedic, I suggest you try this little exercise called "Cutting the Cord."

The idea behind this is that whenever we connect to someone we connect to him or her at the point of our solar plexus, the area just below your diaphragm. When we first meet someone and fall in love, we spend a lot of time building up this energy which lightworkers say looks like a rope of light connecting two people. However, even after one person disappears, the rope can still remain. Often, the person who is left behind spends a lot of time fortifying that rope with his or her own psychic energy in an attempt to bring the person back. The ex can be compared to a psychic vampire gleefully sucking back the energy that the dumped person is sending out. It doesn't matter if you are sending bad thoughts or resentment. To him or her, that energy is often translated in the purest form of astral energy, and used to transmute and feed the new relationship. Thus, in order to prevent yourself being sucked dry by the psychic vampire, I suggest you try this: Lie down on the bed, breathe deeply and become as relaxed as you can. Now picture the other person and the cord of light that you created when you thought the both of you would be connected for all eternity. Visualize that cord as best you can and examine it.

How thick is it? What color is it? What is it made of? Now choose your weapon. What will you use to cut this cord? Do you need a knife or is the connection so strong that it can be broken only by hacking at it with a machete? If a machete doesn't work, try a buzz saw. My favorite weapon is a huge pair of golden scissors. Now, in your mind's eye, snip, hack, chop, sever…do whatever you have to do to cut the cord. Picture the other person floating away from you like a helium balloon let loose in the sky…and smile and wave "bye-bye!" Oddly, one of the side benefits to this ritual is that the other person senses the detachment. Like a villain returning to the scene of the crime, the vampire will return to see where their source of energy has gone. So not only does this exercise your astral health, but it often brings the ex back. That is, if you want them back at all.

The Love Blast Meditation

Believe it or not, you don't always have to fight fire with fire. You can put out a fire with water. The astral equivalent of water is love. It involves visualizing the attacker. If you don't know who it is, you can still ask for loving energy to be sent to the right target. This meditation is good for almost all forms of astral attack that you feel originates from a person—living or dead. It could be an ancestor of yours that harmed you as a child, an overly critical boss, an ex-lover or a spell caster. This one usually throws them for a quite a loop without harming them.

Lie down flat on your back. Close your eyes and cross your hands over your heart. Breathe deeply.

Now imagine there is a pinpoint of light right at your solar plexus. Keep breathing in until this pinpoint of light swells to the size of a glowing yellow star.

Now each time you take a breath, imagine this glowing yellow star sending a stream of energy to another pinpoint of light. This light is in your heart. Right now it is enclosed inside the bud of a flower. Each time you take a breath imagine the petals of this flower unfolding to disclose a rose-colored gem in the center.

Imagine this rose-colored light glowing brighter with each breath. As you breathe in, it emanates a warm pink glow about three feet around your body. For further protection, visualize the entire room you are in filled with this brilliant, rosy pink light. If you concentrate hard enough, you can project this pink light to encompass a whole city block. Project it as far as you can. Surround yourself, your room and your house with this bubble of pink light.

Now visualize the person you suspect of attacking you standing before you. What kind of look does the person have? Is he frowning or scowling? Change that look to a soft smile. Change it to a broad smile. Change it to a look that means that he or she is over-joyed to see you.

Scan the person's body with your imagination. Find the heart.

Now breathing deeply, concentrate on sending him a ray of soft, rose-colored light. Send it directly to the heart, for as long as you can.

When you feel an inner click inside, stop sending the light.

Now smile at the person and wave goodbye. Say "Bless You" in your mind. Tell her you wish her all the happiness she deserves. Visualize the person turning away from you and waving goodbye.

Focus now on your own heart. Concentrate on the petals of the flower. Picture this flower closing over the gem in your heart's center.

Now as you breathe in, concentrate once again on the light in your solar plexus. Imagine this light spreading through your entire body and filling it with gold.

When you are satisfied that your body is filled with gold, say the words "Peace Be Still" and open your eyes.

The Soul-to-Soul Talk

This meditation involves having a heart-to-heart talk with another individual's soul. If a person is filled with hate, resentment, fear or envy or has a dysfunctional personality, sometimes it is easy for you to talk to his or her Higher Self rather than to talk in person. The

Higher Self is devoid of the same characteristics that the personality has, yet it has a subtle influence on the personality. Using this meditation may manifest a sudden change of behavior on the part of the other person with regards to you. It is useful for all forms of attack.

Lie down your flat on your back. Breathe and relax.

Imagine a bright ball of light about three feet above your head. You can actually imagine a being that looks somewhat like you. This is your Higher Self or soul. This is a benevolent, compassionate version of yourself. This is the self that lives in a perfect world. Greet your Higher Self. Imagine your Higher Self smiling and sending you love.

Now imagine another light. This one is hundreds of feet above you. It looks like a burning ball aflame…a small shining sun. It is the purest, whitest light imaginable. This is the Divine Light—the ultimate source of all love and imagination.

As you breathe in, imagine this divine light shooting light downwards and sending it into the ball of light that is just above your head. As you breathe out, see your Higher Self being energized by the light sent from this higher sun.

Now imagine the person that you are having problems with. Visualize him or her from head to toe. Imagine this person is standing right in front of you. Now visualize that this person too, has a little ball of shining light about three feet above his or her head.

Now you are going to create a triangle of light. You are going to imagine that there is a beam of light connecting your Higher Self to the other person's Higher Self. Once you have made this connection, you ask that your Higher Self be allowed to speak to the other person's Higher Self. The person is still facing you. Say what it is you have to say. Explain why the hatred or difference between you needs to be dissolved. Explain why it would be good for you both and everyone else. Keep your words positive: "I would like you to leave me alone because by focusing on me you are reducing your chances of meeting another person."

Now imagine that the shining sun high above you is sending light down to both of your Higher Selves. In your mind's eye you are seeing two people with a triangle of light above both of your heads. The Divine Light is at the top of the triangle.

You ask the divine light to send both of you the love, courage, strength and imagination required to resolve the situation.

Keep up this visualization of the Higher Sun sending light down upon both of you for as long as you can. Remember to keep up the image of the energy flowing back and forth between the two of you at the same time.

When you feel you have sent enough energy, you usually feel a little "click" indicating the matter is done.

Dissolve the image and open your eyes.

The Transmutation of Negative into Positive Energy

This is a breathing exercise intended to purify the aura. It is good for any form of astral attack.

You may do this sitting, standing up or lying down. Imagine yourself surrounded in a bubble of golden light. Breathe deeply from your solar plexus.

Close your mouth. Breathe in with both nostrils. As you breathe imagine that you are inhaling warm yellow light. Open your mouth slightly. As you breathe out, imagine all negativity, tension, resentment, sickness and emotions leaving your body. The breath from your exhalation might seem charcoal-colored, foggy or black....

The moment this dark breath hits the air, imagine it immediately transformed into shining droplets of shimmering gold.

Do this at least ten times.

Positive Affirmations for Replacing Negative Words and Thought Forms

If you are haunted by harsh words or have a fear of negative thought forms you can try repeating the following positive affirmations:

Divine Love now dissolves every thought that is not of itself. There is no more powerful rinsing chemical in the universe than Divine Love. I recognize all that is my good now.

Happiness, joy and soul freedom are mine by Divine Right. I cast this problem to a Higher Power and go free.

No man's will interferes with the flow of Divine Love. There are no obstacles in the Divine Mind; therefore there is nothing to obstruct my good. I am true to heaven's vision for me.

I do not resist this situation. It is in the hands of Divine Love and Wisdom. There is nothing to fear because there is no power to hurt.

I cannot lose anything that is mine by Divine Right, and if I do lose it, then it is replaced by its equal or better. All is well in my world. All is well in all worlds.

Protective Angels

The Archangels can protect you from every single form of astral attack. You can call on them anytime by name and ask them personally for help or you can light a candle and pray.

For Protection: Light a blue candle to the Archangel Michael and ask him to surround you in a protective bubble of blue light. When in danger walking down the street it helps to imagine yourself surrounded by a force field of blue light.

For Peaceful Resolution of Conflict: Light a rose or pink-colored candle to the Archangel Chamuel, the Angel of Love and ask him to blast the situation with Divine Love.

For Disconnection from Astral Attack from an Individual, Ghosts, Spirits or Astral Entities: Light a yellow candle to the Archangel Gabriel, the Angel of Illumination and ask him to remove all hooks and unwanted energies from your third chakra.

For the Healing of Damage to the Aura: Light a green candle and ask the Archangel Rapheal, the Angel of Healing to restore your energy and heal any holes or rips in your aura.

For the Restoration of the Third Eye: Light a red, purple or gold candle (or all three together) to the Archangel Uriel, the Angel of Peace and ask that your intuition be restored. Ask that all the parties involved in the situation be taught to let go of their hostilities.

For the Transformation of Negative Energy into Positive Energy: Pray to the Archangel Zadkiel, the Angel of Joy. Ask that all negative energy that is sent to you be transformed into positive light. Ask him to protect your crown chakra from invasion and unwanted influences and thought forms.

Protective Saints

Appealing to or making a petition to the Saints for assistance against astral attack is a tradition found in Catholicism, Wiccan, Alexandrian, Yoruban, Santerian, Churches of Truth and New Age religions.

Traditionally, the request is written on a small slip of paper and placed under the burning candle. Commercial candles, featuring an image of a Saint on a glass jar filled with wax can be purchased for this purpose.

However, it is my opinion that these candle-burning rituals require nothing more than the lighting of the appropriately colored candle and a short, sincere prayer for help that is directly addressed to the Saint.

Saint Alex: On a Sunday, burn a pink candle and ask for protection against negative thought forms and the harm your enemies might wish to send you.

Saint Barbara: On a Saturday, light a red candle to ward off all evil, protect against astral interference, clear your path of obstacles and ask for protection against binding or black magic.

Saint Cipriano: On a Saturday, light a purple candle and ask for protection from black magic. He also protects against bad neighbors, liars, cheaters, addicts, bad coincidences, man-made disasters and natural disasters.

Saint Clare of Assisi: On a Monday, light a white candle and ask for protection from alcoholics, mentally ill people and psychic invaders. She can also assist you with your own temptations.

Saint Dymphna: On a Monday, light a blue candle to help with obsession, possession by demons, nervous disorders and astral attack from the living or the dead.

Our Lady of Fatima: On a Tuesday, light a white candle and pray for protection from binding situations, spells and evil spirits.

Saint Francis of Assisi: On a Monday, light a brown candle and ask him for protection against secret plots, conspiracies and cults.

Saint Gerard Magella: On a Monday, light a white candle for overall astral protection as well as protection while channelling, healing or practicing mediumship.

Saint Ignatius of Loyala: On a Saturday, light a white candle and ask for assistance in ridding a house of evil spirits, entities or ghosts.

Saint John The Baptist: On a Tuesday, light a green candle and ask for protection from astral enemies or anything or anyone that shakes your faith.

Saint Jude: On any day light green, white and red candles together when trapped in what seems a hopeless or desperate situation.

Saint Lucy of Syracuse: On a Wednesday, light a white candle and ask for temptations to be conquered, obstacles cleared and protection from the evil eye.

Saint Louis Beltran: On any day light a white candle to remove the evil eye from children.

Saint Philomena: On a Saturday, light a pink or green candle and ask this patroness of desperate situations to cleanse you from all evil thought forms and to restore your soul.

Saint Martin Caballero: On any day light a red and white candle together to block obstacles and black magic, rescue someone from evil influences or ask for release from demonic possession.

Saint Rita of Cascia: On a Sunday, light a white candle and ask for deliverance from abusive relationships. She also helps restore faith and gives you patience.

Saint Therese of Lisieux: On a Wednesday, light a yellow candle and petition her for protection against addicts and for protection from harm from enemies using black magic.

Protective Psalms

Reading from the Bible or any sacred text is supposed to provide powerful protection from astral attack. The repetition of holy words strengthens the aura and repels invasion. The Psalms suggested below may help with a given situation:

For Protection Against the Wicked: Psalms 10, 12, 64 and 123

To Break a Curse: Psalm 7

To Cause Evil Doers to do Good: Psalm 17

To Cleanse the Mind and Heart: Psalm 119

To Confuse Those Who are Attacking: Psalm 83

Protection from All Enemies: Psalm 18

Deliverance from an Unjust Situation: Psalm 43

Against the Evil Eye: Psalm 36

Discourage Entities and Spirits: Psalm 118

Exorcise Demons: Psalm 29

Exorcise an Evil Spirit: Psalm 68

Protect Against Evil Influences: Psalm 24

Subdue Astral Attack: Psalm 28

Protective Ritual Baths

Sea Salt Bath
The classic remedy for an attack on the aura is to take a bath in sea salts. Epsom salts will do the trick too, but I personally think sea salt is the most effective. Put about a 1/4 to 1/2 of a cup of sea salts into a bath half filled with tepid water. Immerse yourself in this bath for at least ten minutes, making sure to fully wet your face and head. When you are done this bath, do not rinse off the salt. Pat yourself dry and go to bed. This bath has the effect of strengthening your electromagnetic field as well as cleansing it from any toxic energy.

Beer Bath
To remove the evil eye, a curse or an astral attack, add one quarter of a cup beer, a squeeze of lemon juice and a handful of sea salt to your bath. If you don't want to use beer you can also use one of the Mud Hops bubble baths on the market, many of which already contain the lemon as well. To this you can toss in a handful of sea salt. Stay in this bath for at least fifteen minutes and then rinse off.

Barley Water Bath
This is for protection and to dispel evil with a capital E. This is definitely the bath to have if you are feeling haunted by something unseemly and of supernatural origin. Boil whole barley until it is soft in a pot. Drain and save the water. Pour into the bath. Bad spirits will run like hell.

Coconut Obsession-Breaking Milk Bath

You can buy a commercial preparation that is a bubble bath, but the traditional way is to crack a coconut in half and pour half the milk in the water. Take the other half of the coconut milk and pour it directly over your head. This cools and cleanses a disturbed and agitated mind as well as clears attachments. Add a squeeze of lime to this bath if you are feeling a loss of self-control.

Lime Bath for Obsession

Once again, there are many "lime-flavored" shower gels, soaps and bubble baths on the market that will do the job, but squeezing the juice of one lime in the bath is also a classic remedy for obsession.

Protective and Cleansing Gemstones

The New Age should also be called The Stone Age, because along with aromatherapy, healing with the vibrations and frequencies emitted by gemstones is at the crux of the movement. Below I have listed seven popular gemstones, that also correspond with the divine energies of the Seven Archangels. Chances are that many of you own jewelry already set with the following precious gems. If you don't own any jewelry, you can obtain inexpensive, raw and unpolished stones in stores or on the Internet. Once you have the stone, it is best to wear it someplace on your body, like in a necklace, bracelet or ring. You also might want to practice psychometry, which is the intuitive art of holding the stone and sensing its vibration. Some people like to purify raw or unpolished stones, after they have purchased them, by dropping it in a glass of salt for a night. In the case of used jewelry or inherited things, you might want to do this to cleanse it of the energies of the previous owner.

Sapphire: This stone, which is usually the color of the deep, blue sea, will help give you power, focus and determination. It is a great stone to wear when you feel yourself losing hope, stamina and perseverance. A sapphire improves your concentration and helps you stay centered throughout your daily activities. Further, the sapphire corresponds to the energies of the Archangel Michael, who assists us with mental clarity and protects us from accidents. This is a good stone to wear if you are entering a potentially violent, risky or daring situation. It is also a good gem to wear while you are driving.

Yellow Topaz: This clear yellow gem is the "problem solving stone." It is for those who feel overwhelmed by life. You might have that existential feeling like there is no way out of a situation. Use this stone to help you reconnect with your Higher Self, as well as feel physically and emotionally "human" again. The yellow topaz is used by healers to protect themselves from toxic energies and also to release those who feel oppressed by drunken or abusive partners. It can also help obsessive people learn to let go. Wearing topaz helps you connect to the energies of the Archangel Jophiel, who is the Angel of Divine Inspiration.

Rose Quartz: This light pink crystal heals the heart and promotes a sense of self-appreciation and self-love. It also helps you open your heart's center so that you can give love, unconditionally. It protects you against the cruel criticisms of others and unsolicited judgments that act as astral invasion. The rose quartz corresponds to the benevolent energies of the

Archangel Chamuel, the Angel of Love. This is the angel that ensures your survival and removes astral obstacles.

Diamond: Clarity is the key word to describe the uses of a diamond for psychological healing. The diamond is also a stone of communication and aids those who often feel left out to communicate clearly with others. It is good for those who feel consistently misunderstood or like they are socially invisible.

Diamonds have traditionally symbolized the commitment of one human being to another, but in this case they also symbolize a commitment to taking care of your Higher Self. The stone vibrates at a frequency that strengthens your intuitive abilities. It helps you perceive beyond surface appearance and understand the truth about another person. It protects against negation.

Psychologically, wearing a diamond can help you manifest what you want in your life—bringing airy-fairy ideals down into physical reality. This stone is excellent for artists, visionaries and inventors.

The diamond connects you to the peaceful energies of the Archangel Gabriel, who helps you harmonize conflicts in your life on both the physical and astral plane.

Emerald: This brilliant green stone is used to restore balance. Healers use this as an anti-stress stone, and to restore harmony to troubled or split personalities. It is good for manic-depressives, drama queens and others who go to emotional extremes.

If you have a problem with the opposite sex, the emerald can help restore the yin-yang energies in your own body and acknowledge your shadow side. It helps to heal common wounds of the heart such as unrequited love, abandonment and death. It is also used to heal emotional upsets.

At the cellular level, the emerald is thought to restore balance. It is thought to reconnect communication between the left and right brain.

Wearing this stone connects you to the divine energies of the Archangel Raphael—the Angel of Healing. It can clarify and restore your aura and keep your vibration operating at a level where you are beyond astral attack.

Ruby: The blood-red light of the ruby helps to dispel feelings of discouragement and self-doubt and infuse your heart, mind and aura with the qualities of success, affluence, attractiveness and personal victory.

This is the stone to wear if you feel like you are drowning in self-pity. It dispels negative self-talk and is thought to increase confidence and beauty. Wear it if you feel like you are isolated and would like to participate more in your community. It can help you achieve a vibrant social life and attract the right friends. It teaches you to love, give and share with others out of a genuine sense of philanthropy and caring.

The ruby corresponds to the Archangel Uriel, the angel responsible for helping you let go of the forces of anti-love such as resentment, jealousy and bitterness so that fresher, loving and abundant forces can take their place. The ruby is a powerful stone that averts the gaze of the evil eye.

Amethyst: This beautiful purple stone helps you let go of past hurts and relationships. If you are a control freak, this is the gem that will help you "Let go and Let God." It will teach you to trust others and delegate tasks. If you are a meddling type, it will also help you to stop gossiping and mind your own business.

The amethyst has the effect of clearing up the clutter in your life. If you suffer from nightmares, wear an amethyst; it will help release fears and anxieties that might be lurking in your subconscious. It helps reduce tension and stress in the body.

The amethyst aids those who are afraid of experiencing the death process or who cannot move beyond the stage of mourning. It is excellent for those who believe that they are at the mercy of negative thought forms.

Wearing an ameythst helps you to access the energies of the Archangel Zadkiel—the Angel of Joy. This is the angel that transmutes negative energy into positive light.

Other helpful stones are:

Amber absorbs negative energy and transforms it into positive energy, calms nerves and heals.

Bloodstone cleanses the aura, grounds those who are spacey and forces them to live in the here and now rather than in other worlds.

Carnelian dispels laziness, rage, jealousy, envy and fear. It assists actors and writers, inciting creativity.

Citrine aligns and cleans the aura.

Coral connects an individual to spirit guides and offers protection against the evil eye.

Hematite absorbs negative energy from the aura.

Labradorite repairs shattered auras and protects against leaks and holes.

Lodestones reinforce the auric shield.

Obsidian helps ground, protect and dispel negative thoughts and obsessions. It raises self-esteem.

Opal brings out the best in you. It helps you act from the heart. It protects from nightmares.

Pyrite brings psychic protection. It also protects

healers from picking up energies and thought forms from clients.

Quartz (clear) balances your energy field, restores harmony and intuition, and cleanses the aura.

Selenium repels entities and spirits so they can't attach themselves to you.

Tourmaline protects against astral attack.

Turquoise improves communication, intuition, creativity, protection and wisdom, and restores the aura.

Clearing a Space of Bad Vibrations

Feng Shui
According to traditional rules in Feng Shui, clutter attracts bad spirits and blocks the positive flow of energy. If you feel haunted or overly attached to the past, one remedy might be to give your house a good cleaning. If the object feels wrong, or reminds you from the past in a negative way then throw it out. It is also said that Venus, the Goddess of Love, will not empty a dirty home.

Bells and Chimes
Hanging chimes in front of a window or a porch is supposed to prevent bad spirits from entering a house.

Another way of clearing your space is to walk through it, ringing a bell that chimes in the key of C. Balinese temple bells were created exactly for this purpose.

Making a Clean Sweep
A Wiccan tradition for clearing vibrations out of a house is to take a broom and, starting at the front

door, sweep the entire house in a counter-clockwise direction. Even if your floors are clean you can do this as a symbolic action. Keep sweeping in the counter-clockwise direction until you have reached the front door and sweep everything you have collected out the front door and to the edge of the street. Modernists could probably use a vacuum cleaner to the same effect.

Copper Pennies
Four copper pennies placed in the North, South, East and West corners of the house are thought to prevent the inhabitants from astral attack, ghosts and spirits.

Incense
The classic incense used for protection is a combination of frankincense and myrrh, which is said to please the angels and summon protective light. Genuine frankincense and myrrh can be bought in religious supply stores and burned over charcoal in an incense burner. The burner is swung through the house, cleansing every corner of thought forms, entities and bad energy. In Arab homes today, on Thursdays, frankincense is burned in a censer and carried through each room to expel evil spirits and invite the angels in. In Cairo, Egypt, people earn their livelihood by traveling from business to business, burning this combination of incense to dispel any negative energy left behind by the public.

Sage can also be used to purify an environment. It can be bought commercially as stick incense or as a sage bundle. A bundle is usually just the dried herb wrapped with an elastic band or rope. The bundle is lit on fire and carried through the house to clear it of entities and bad spirits. In several Native American cultures, the aroma of burning sweet grass or sage purifies the energies and attracts positive supernatural entities.

The burning of bay leaves is a tradition from ancient Greece that was not only thought to bring prosperity but also to keep inauspicious energies literally at bay.

Burning rosemary incense is thought to keep witches away and invite the benevolent protective hand of the Virgin Mary into your environment.

In Wiccan traditions, rue is often burned to protect against entities and negative thought forms and to get energy flowing in a positive direction again.

Protective Herbs

Herbs can be worn on the person, sprinkled about the home, hidden in a potpourri, burned as incense, bathed in or simmered in a pot. Here is a compendium of herbs that protect against invasion and psychic attack.

Agrimony: Acts as a deflective shield and sends bad vibrations back to their source.

Angelica: A highly protective herb said to summon the angels. In its tea form, it can be sprinkled in a few corners of a house to keep evil away.

Anise: Raises vibrations to the highest possible psychic level. Good for bringing about changes in attitude (refocusing). Stuffed inside a pillow, it is said to keep away nightmares that could be caused by astral attack.

Asafetida: One of the foulest smelling and strongest of the protective herbs. Traditionally it was used in exorcism and purification rituals to drive away evil and destroy manifestations.

Bay Leaves: Powerful protective herb used for banishing evil spirits and ghosts.

Betony: A banishing herb used for removing negative energy.

Bindweed: Used in both hexing and protection to stop an astral attack, and as the rope in binding rituals.

Blueberry: Used for both hexing and protection as it guards against deception and secrecy.

Camphor: Used to cleanse and banish all forms of psychic aggression.

Capsicum (Cayenne Pepper): Used to reverse evil and return it to the sender.

Cedar: Protects mediums and channelers from psychic attack while the Third Eye is open. In some cultures, the oil is used to anoint the Third Eye before meditation.

Deer's Tongue: Used to diagnose possession and reveal the presence of bad energy.

Dragon's Blood: Used in rituals for psychic power and astral protection.

Elm bark: Eliminates slander, gossip, criticism and bad thought forms.

Eucalyptus: Used to cleanse an environment of bad spirits.

Fennel: Used to remove hexes.

Geranium: Banishes negativity and gloomy vibes. Very protective. Used to heal the aura of rips and tears due to astral attack.

Hawthorn: Used for protection, purification and banishing rituals.

Hazel: Used to put a damper on envy, jealousy and resentment.

Heather: Protects against elemental spirits.

Hyacinth: Used to replace negative vibes with positive ones.

Lavender: Cleanses, protects and shields from bad vibrations and negativity, particularly from an ex-lover.

Lemon Verbena: Converts negative energy into positive. Cleanses negative vibrations.

Lily of the valley: Used for calming spirits and blessing an enviroment.

Marjoram: Used for protecting a family or a house from evil spirits and bad luck in general.

Mistletoe: Used since ancient times for protection.

Motherwort: Used for astral protection in general.

Myrtle: Hung on front doors for protection against psychic aggression.

Pennyroyal: Cleanses and protects the family home and clears away spirits that might be causing family arguments.

Pine: Repairs shattered auras, clears negative thought forms and aids channelers in focusing.

Rosemary: Used for purification and protection of the home.

Rue: Highly protective. Guards against negative energies and forces stagnant energy to move in a positive direction. Thaws frozen energy and breaks binding spells.

St. John's Wort: Rapidly reverses animosity between people. Grounds and dispels negative energies.

Sandalwood: Used to heighten spiritual vibrations, to cleanse, heal and protect.

Sassafras: Used to free you of another's power over you.

Slippery Elm: Protects against gossip or slander and the evil eye.

Snakeroot: Use when you want to be rid of a person or thing. Disconnects individuals at the astral level.

Thyme: Raises vibrations to a higher level and encourages the practical application of spiritual principles in life. Used for protection against psychic invasion and psychic vampires.

Vetivert (khus khus): Used for removal of bad spirits and refocusing of the Third Eye. Replaces negative thought forms with positive ones.

Bells, Whistles and Other Methods of Spirit Wrangling

Spirits don't like noise. They don't like hustle, bustle and rooms full of people. They can't feed off negativity if none is there.

If you feel like a ghost, spirit or entity inhabits your home, one way to get rid of it is to walk through the house banging pots and pans loudly. You can also ring bells, blow whistles, clap your hands—anything to make a racket for five minutes.

Spirits and entities can be attracted to music, particularly melancholy music but they are not that fond of the television. One way to ward off attacks from the otherworld is to keep the television and radio on all day.

Keep your environment as cheery and noisy as possible. They will attach to gloom and doom elsewhere.

Asking Politely

If you do happen to think your home is inhabited by a spirit, entity or ghost, you might try directly communicating with them. Many are not as malevolent as they seem. They are simply lost. Most of these other-worldly beings are said to have a somewhat zombie-like character that readily responds to commands. One idea might be to meditate and see if you can communicate with what is there. If you feel some kind of connection, then ask politely for the spirit to go back from where it came. You might also thank it for the visit, explain why it has to go and request that it please leave. Many ghostbusters have had astounding success with performing this simple and courteous procedure.

You can also try this with any form of psychic aggression, especially if you feel that it originates from a person you know. For instance, if you suffer from an unpleasant memory or thought, you can always say "No thank you. It's my brain and I will let what I want into it. Go back to where you came from! Thank you!"

Chapter Four

The Cures for Astral Attack:
The Velvet Fist

The rituals in this chapter are a little tougher than the ones in the last and involve the use of magic. I do not often do these rituals myself, as they do not follow the principles of non-resistance, however some readers may find them helpful depending on the situation.

Lesser Banishing Pentagram Ritual

The Lesser Banishing Ritual is Qabalistic in origin, but practiced in many pagan and New Age religions to banish bad energy. Many versions of this ritual exist; the one below has been simplified.

Also known as the Archangel Purification Ritual, this performance invokes the Archangels to bless or clear a space of old or negative energies. It is considered to be extremely protective against all forms of attack and invasion.

Part 1: Perform the Qabalistic Cross
1. Touch the forehead with your hand and say "ATOH" (Thou art).
2. Touch the mid-point of the breast and say "MALKUS" (the Kingdom).
3. Touch the left shoulder and say "VE-GEDU-LAH" (and the Glory).
4. Touch the right shoulder and say "VE-GE-VURAH" (and the Power).
5. Interlace your fingers and place your clasped hands on the breast, and say "LE-OLAHM AMEN" (forever, Amen).

Part 2: Face East
1. Stretch out the right hand with the index and middle finger extended and the thumb clasping the ring finger and pinky. Some practitioners imagine a cleansing blue light emits from this finger positioning.
2. Visualize a large blue pentagram that extends to your arm's width in the air before you. Trace the pentagram with your finger in the air. Make the first point of the star at the bottom left-hand corner; the second point the top point of the star; the third point down to the right; then, continue up to the left, straight across to the right and then down again to the original starting point on the left until you have completed the star shape.
3. Chant the word "YHVH" (Pronounced YOD-HEH-VAV-HEH). Imagine the star is glowing a bright yellow.

Part 3: Face South
1. Trace another pentagram in the air using your index and forefinger in precisely the same way as above.
2. Chant the word "ADNI" (AH-DOH-NAI) and visualize the pentagram glowing red.

Part 4: Face West
1. Trace another pentagram in the air using your index and forefinger as described above.
2. Chant "AHIH" (EH-HE-YEH) and imagine a blazing blue pentagram.

Part 5: Face North
1. Trace another pentagram as described above.
2. Chant "AGLA" (AH-GE-LAH) and visualize a green pentagram.

Part 6: Face East Again

1. Use your forearms and hands to form the shape of a cross.

2. Say:

"Before me Raphael,
Behind me Gabriel,
On my right hand Michael,
On my left hand Ariel,
For before me flames the Pentagram,
And behind me shines the six-rayed Star."

Part 7: Repeat the Qabalistic Cross

Now go to Starbucks and have a café latte.

Basic Candle Burning

This kind of protective magic can be done at any time, but is especially effective when done during a waning moon (the fourteen-day period when the moon is going from full to new).

Some sign phases are more suited to reversal magic than others. If you wish your ritual to affect someone profoundly on the unconscious level, perform the candle burning when the moon is waning in the astrological sign of Pisces.

For rapid results, do the ritual when the moon is waning in Aries or Gemini. To achieve justice or simply what is fair for all, do the ritual when the moon is waning in Libra. Candle burning performed when the moon is waning in Leo or Scorpio often manifests in dramatic or severe results.

Usually you buy smaller candles and let them burn down over a period of hours on your chosen night.

Brown Candle: Is used for grounding and protection, and to repel negative vibrations.

Green and Black Candle Together: Used to return jealousy, greed, suspicion and resentment back to its source.

Red and Black Candle Together: Used to send hatred, violence, revenge and cruelty back to its source.

White and Black Candle Together: For basic reversal of karma. Sends all bad energy back to its source.

Blue and Black Candle Together: Used to send negative emotions, melancholy and obsessive thoughts that you believe do not belong to you back to their source.

Specific Reversal Spells

To Protect From a Jinxed Condition
A purple candle, anointed with the commercially sold Uncrossing Oil. Place a piece of paper or parchment with your request written on it beneath the candle.

To Reverse a Curse to Known and Unknown Enemies
This is a black and red candle burned together or a commercially sold Reversible Candle in a glass jar, and dressed with Dragon's Blood Oil. Write your name in the wax at the top.

To Gain Spiritual Strength
Write your name on a white candle, anoint with a dab of olive oil and burn it.

To Clear a Home or Space of Negative Energies
Light a blue candle and anoint it with olive oil. If you know who is causing the trouble, write their names

on a piece of paper nine times and place it beneath the candle.

Binding Spell
Technically under the category of black magic, this spell comes in handy when one is confronted with a violent abuser or a known attacker.

Take an object that represents the individual. The best is a photograph. If a photograph is not available draw images and words on a piece of paper or cardboard that represent the evil situation or person that you wish to bind. You may also bind energies that you sense are around such as greed, jealously, envy and disrespect.

Take a length of black or red yarn (or both) and wind it around the object twenty-one times. For each loop you string around the cardboard, say one line of the following chant:

"With the thread of the crimes
Spun from your mind
I bind your evil
Three time seven times.
I bind you from Behind
I bind you from Before
You won't hurt yourself or me
Anymore
I bind you from the Left
I bind you from the Right
I bind you by Day
And I bind you by Night.
I bind you from Below
I bind you from Above
That you may finally know
The laws of karma and love

I bind you with
The Guilt Within
May you know what you have done
As I ravel, so your secrets unravel
Let this binding begin. . . ."

Tie off the ends of the yarn with three sturdy knots to seal the spell.

If you are using a photograph, seal it between two pocket mirrors so the person can take a good look at his or her own behavior. If you are using cardboard or paper, either store it in a safe place or burn it.

Freezer Spell

This is also technically black magic as it dominates another's will (another's will to do you harm, mind you) but it is relatively benign in its intent.

Fill a container three-quarters full of water. Write the offender's name on a piece of paper. If you don't know who is attacking you write "unknown attacker." Stick the piece of paper in the container. Now fill the rest of the container with one or all of the following ingredients: sugar, honey, maple syrup, sweetener, vanilla, saccharin or Sweet 'N Low. If you want to soften them up, throw in some MSG as well. Cap the container and throw it in the freezer. Leave it there until you feel their attitude towards you is a little sweeter.

Bad Energy in a Bottle

If you know who your attacker is, take a small photograph of them or write his or her name on a piece of paper. Stick this object in a bottle and cork it. Visualize that person's bad energy trapped in the bottle. Put an expiration date on it. Store in a cool, dark place.

Protection Using Ancestral Spirits
This simple ritual involves building an altar to your deceased ancestors that consists of photographs of them. Burn a white candle and ask them to protect you from psychic invasion.

Creating a Guardian
This is a spiritual matter that depends largely on your ability to creatively visualize the following: a beast, person from history, a god or goddess, mythological creature, weapon and/or fortress.

In this instance what you are doing is subconsciously creating a being or a form that will protect you on the astral plane.

Most people create guardians that are animals or beasts. One way to start this process is to consider your ancestry and some of the totem animals that might be related to you. For instance if you are Nordic, you might find yourself imagining a protective animal that looks like a white wolf. Some people create guardians that look like mythical animals, such as a cross between a cat and a monkey, or a lion and an eagle. Once you have imagined this creation in every detail, you are to set it to guard the portal of your subconscious, so that it terrifies all of those who might attempt unauthorized entry.

Other individuals may take their cue form history and imagine a soldier, warrior or goddess such as Alexander the Great, Ghengis Kahn or Hathor.

Another technique is to imagine yourself surrounded by a fortress that is decorated with gargoyles and filled with booby traps.

Some psychics imagine weapons. If someone tries to invade their consciousness, they imagine a cannon, gun or beam of light is pointed at the enemy to warn them of unauthorized entry.

Perhaps the simplest of these visualizations is to imagine your psyche as a temple with a locked door. Anyone who tries to get in will be confronted with a doorknob that won't turn, or a door that only opens from the inside.

The key to this one is to use your imagination and what feels right to you.

Protective Symbols, Charms and Totems

There is power in old images and symbols. Below is a compendium of common symbols, charms and totems from antiquity that are thought to be useful against psychic aggression. These items can be worn, carried (talisman) or placed in the home (sculpture).

Abracadabra: One of the oldest protective amulets, it is written in a triangular form and thought to protect against injustice and evil events:

A
AB
ABRA
ABRAC
ABRACA
ABRACAD
ABRACADA
ABRACADAB
ABRACADABR
ABRACADABRA

Bast: This is usually represented by the image of a black cat. In ancient Eygpt, Bast or Bastet was thought to protect home and family from negative spiritual influences.

Cancer: The astrological symbol of Cancer, the Crab, is thought to protect against astral attack.

Celtic Cross: A crucifix within a circle, this ancient symbol is thought to protect from spiritual dangers of all kinds.

Celtic Knots: These rings of circles created from interwoven bands appear in all kinds of intricate forms and designs. One of their primary functions is to protect against wicked plots, group magic, evil spirits and demons.

Devil's Snare or Trap: This is a circle of Hebraic writing that spirals inward in a counter-clockwise direction. The idea is that evil spirits become trapped in the coil of writing. It is Assyrian in origin and thought to protect against sorcery and all evil.

The Dog: A Native American talisman against astral attacks. He stands at the doors of the other-world and prevents spirits from attacking the living.

The Elk: A symbol of psychic self-defence and protection, the rune of the Elk (known as Algiz) is worn to defend against spirits and make one brave while facing fear of the unknown.

Eye of Horus: An important protective symbol in ancient Egypt, it helps guard against the evil eye.

The Falcon: A North American symbol of perception that represents the high perch of elevated spirituality. It enhances astral abilities so one is able to perceive negative energy and make it one's metaphorical prey.

Fish: In Native American cultures, the fish represents a refusal to recognize the power of another's magic.

The Frog: A North American symbol indicating mediumship. It is thought to cleanse and purify the aura.

Griffin: Most griffins feature the body of a lion and the head of an eagle. Some have wings. This mythical being, Grecian in origin, is said to protect the psyche from dark forces.

Hagal: This protective rune looks like an H, represents hail and protects from all attacks and misfortunes including astral attack.

Ingwaz: This rune resembles a diamond shape and represents an egg. It is protective against the evil eye and astral attack.

Isa: The symbol of an I that represents Ice. It is thought to increase personal shamanic powers as well as protect one from evil influences and undesirable astral forces.

Jaguar: The Mayan symbol of the jaguar is thought to protect against control freaks, evil thought forms and to increase one's own shamanistic abilities.

The Lucky Hand: Many variations of this exist from all cultures. Usually, this symbol features the palm of a hand facing out. In the center of the palm may be a pentagram, an eye, a gemstone or a Zodiac sign. It is thought to protect against all forms of astral invasion and attack. It is especially effective against ritual abuse.

Mannaz: This protective rune resembles an M and represents the Higher Self. It protects against interference with one's connection to their intuition and God.

The Mitzu Domo: This symbol is Japanese and features three whirling swirl shapes. It is thought to protect against the impatience, greed and acceleration of time associated with astral attacks.

Mother Gaia: This is usually the figure of a goddess with her hands reaching in a circle above her head.

She protects against disturbances to our auras and helps ground our energy

The Om Symbol: This ancient Sanskrit symbol represents the syllable "om" that is used in meditation. It raises one's vibration so that the aura cannot be reached by the baser energies associated with psychic aggression.

The Pentagram: Also known as the Druid's foot, this six-sided star protects against witchcraft and the evil eye. It is thought to return bad energy back to the sender.

Pictic Knot: This Celtic symbol that features an interlocking series of triangles protects against magical rites that have gone wrong and missed their aim.

The Raven: A Native American and Celtic symbol thought to protect against black magic.

Sagittarius: The astrological symbol of the Archer is thought to protect against psychic vampires and those who deplete spiritual energy.

Scorpio: The astrological symbol of Scorpio, the Scorpion, is thought to protect against witchcraft, the evil eye and the kind of fanaticism associated with cults and ritual attack.

The Seal of Solomon: One of the best known protective symbols, this features two interlocking triangles that form a star shape. It is used to invoke the Archangels and protect against black magic and the power of all evil.

Solomon's Seal Charm Amulet: This amulet features the number 10 in the center and is decorated with the number 100 written in several alphabets. The word OM appears twelve times around its borders. It protects against black magic, witchcraft, psychic vampires, inner unrest, ghosts and spirits.

Suli: This is a Celtic amulet that depicts the Sun God in a halo of flames. He protects against spiritual weakness.

The Sun: The universal symbol of the sun is worn to oppose its shadow or dark energy. It is common to all cultures.

Thor's Hammer: This symmetrical three-pronged knot protects against malfortune, the evil eye and those who would rob the spirits.

The Turtle: Helps one remain invisible to others on the astral plane.

Uruz: This Nordic rune looks like an upside down U and represents an ox. It helps one connect to their Higher Self and protects against astral attack. It is thought to help one remain grounded spiritually.

Virgo: The astrological symbol of Virgo, the Virgin, is thought to protect against cults, covens and groups that do not encourage soul freedom.

The Wolf: A Northern European and Native American symbol that protects against astral attack.

The Yew Tree: Increases endurance and power, and is thought to protect against deception, betrayal, delusion, undesirable influences and thought forms. The rune that symbolizes the yew tree (known as Eiwaz), is worn as a protective talisman.

Chapter Five

The Art of Transmutation

In the last two chapters I describe what I would call "Magic Monkeys," in order to defy psychic aggression. Although these can be effective for some people, I personally believe that a connection to the Divine Source of Power—God, Buddha, Mohammed, Goddess, whatever—is there for all to access without these tools. Most of the time I don't believe you need a high priest, guru or channeler to solve your problems.

Also, I am personally sickened by astral wars. The astral plane is polluted by individuals creating more karma by constantly reversing negativity and sending it back to the original sender. If the sender retaliates, then even more negative energy is created causing a dramatic build up of negative energy which has nowhere to go. The ideal solution is to try to resist the temptation to fight fire with fire and send the energy heavenward for God to take care of (where humans can't touch it) or try to transform its polarity to positive energy.

Transmutation is the spiritual art of raising your personal vibration so that it is so high no form of astral aggression can reach you. The more you achieve enlightenment, the less you are affected by thought forms, sour emotions, fear, envy, resentment, retribution, the Seven Deadly Sins, covens, cults, religious programing, unwanted mental influences, rituals, spells, curses and everything else that we call evil in this world.

A deflated soul can be compared to deflated tires on a car. The less air in the tires, the more we feel every bump on the road. The idea is to inflate your spiritual tires so that you do not feel every obstacle on your spiritual journey. You are above the fray of corruption.

Raising your vibration does not require a program of intense spiritual study, knowledge of the wisdom of the ages or the guidance of a shaman. All that it requires is the ability to release your burdens to your Higher Power. There is no higher power than the Divine Love and Guidance that we receive from that Great Being of Love up there every day. One of the most powerful things you can do, in a desperate or hopeless situation, is surrender the problem to the God that is within you. This gives you the faith and confidence that you will be able to handle whatever comes your way in the future.

Part of this is making an agreement with yourself that there is nothing in this world that has the power to influence, attack or invade your Higher Self. There is a time in one's life when one must learn to throw away the "Magic Monkeys" and practice the law of non-resistance to events.

It is our own fears that cause the most damage to our auras. The key to the law of non-resistance is to not be afraid of the monsters that we perceive in real life or the astral plane. Facing our fears is the surest way to diminish their powers over us.

The fine art of transmutation is learning to change negative energy into positive energy simply by changing our perspective and attitude. Part of this change might involve walking right into the lion's den and facing our biggest fears. Half the time we find out these lions are nothing but a litter of pussycats.

Each of us, in essence, contains a hologram of God or the Divine Source. Some say this hologram of God is in our Third Eye. The idea is to realize that we are always perfect, whole and complete, regardless of the interference of others. Most of what we perceive as interference is actually our own fears and resentments manifesting in the external world. What is reflected back to us is not always the truth of the matter.

If you are suffering from an astral attack, you might want to consider what it is that you are doing to manifest such a phenomenon. If you are an astral codependent, chances are that souls (dead or alive) are seeking you because you are constantly seeking connection with them. The idea is not to put any effort into the idea of being a seeker of anything. You are to live in the moment and as the cliché goes, "accept the present as a gift." Most astral attacks originate from a place of distorted expectations and fears of the future in both the sender and the victim. Negative vibrations cluster together like a forest of tuning forks. The idea is to raise your vibrations so high, that even the Hounds from Hell can't hear the sound.

Through a personal commitment to your physical, spiritual and mental health you can successfully cleanse your aura. You can develop the ease and lack of effort that it takes to accomplish true detachment from other people's emotions and situations. Although being a psychic sponge sounds romantic, the image almost ultimately guarantees that you will be a doormat (a perpetual victim) in life.

There are many reasons and justifications to stay engaged in astral battle. You can tell yourself it is necessary because the other person is your soulmate. You can tell yourself it is an absolute because it is dictated by karma. You can blame it on fate.

However, achieving a state of spiritual poise and grace absolves you from all of those conditions. Many cannot handle the sobriety from human drama that enlightenment entails—they are addicted to being self-serious. If there is one thing that I know is true, we were not put here to wring our hands, wail and make things harder for ourselves. Also humor destroys karma, almost as easily as Divine Love. A child's giggle can clear a room of negative energies faster than candles, incense, positive affirmations and the Lesser Banishing Ritual of the Pentagram.

Once you have transcended the banality of evil, simply by not recognizing its effects on you, you will develop the ability naturally, to transform all negative energy into positive energy. A jump-start visualization for this is to imagine yourself casting all your burdens, trials and problems into a violet flame, that consumes and transforms them into a brilliant golden energy.

Practicing the law of non-resistance takes some faith. For this reason I have chosen to end this book with one of the most powerful prayers in the world "The Prayer of Saint Francis of Assisi." It is one of your ultimate weapons against astral attack.

"O Lord, make me an instrument of Thy Peace!
Where there is hatred, let me sow love;
Where there is injury, pardon;
Where there is discord, harmony;
Where there is doubt, faith;
Where there is despair, hope;
Where there is darkness, light, and
Where there is sadness, joy.
O Divine Master, grant that I may not so much

seek to be consoled as to console; to be understood as to understand; to be loved as to love; For it is in giving that we receive, it is in pardoning that we are pardoned, and it is in dying that we are born to Eternal Life.
Amen."

You can pray that again!